Serving Donuts is not Sales

At what point do we, those of us who are professional sales people or, as I call us, "peddlers," (not clerks, sales associates or tellers), defend who we are? **THIS IS THAT POINT**!

For me, it was time to ask why one of the world's highest paid professions has never gotten the respect it deserves. Lets face it, we live in the best neighborhoods, drive the best cars, send our children to the finest schools. Yet, the neighbors, especially those who are doctors, lawyers, bank presidents and so forth, seem to look down their professional noses at us. And, the people whom we sell to treat us as if we have never earned a single dime of what we have. Why?

Why do clerks call themselves salespeople? At what point do we differentiate between the professional peddler who prepares, plans and executes and the clerk, working at the local 7-11 who claims to have "sold" two dozen glazed donuts that morning.

This book is going to identify the real peddlers out there and will help those who have the talent and, above all else, the courage to go out and make their living by pursuing a career as sales professionals. At the same time, it is going to narrow the field by illustrating clearly why many of you who think sales is easy, are dead wrong.

SERVING DONUTS IS NOT SALES

A unique way of looking
at the world's highest paid
profession by someone who
has absolutely been there

By

Lee Klein

First published by AuthorHouse 10/05/05

ISBN: 1-4208-8068-3 (sc)
ISBN: 1-4208-8478-6 (dj)

Library of Congress Control Number: 2005907721

Printed in the United States of America
Bloomington, Indiana

This book is printed on acid-free paper.

DEDICATED TO ...

I suppose that every book or piece of writing needs to be dedicated to someone. At least, every book I have ever read had a dedication.

This book is being dedicated as the very last thing that I do in relation to this work. I have completed this ten-year-long, on–again, off-again project that has seen me relocate, change careers, turn 50 years old at the beginning, and 60 at the end.

I now want to make sure that I dedicate this effort to someone very special to me. I have known and worked for (and with) some exceptional, very famous people who, in every case, would be more than worthy of this personal tribute. I have had a few, but not many, heroes as I have held that term "hero" in a very special place for a very special few. I was fortunate enough to have a wonderful mother and father, each of whom would deserve and could easily get this dedication. And I am one of the fortunate few who has sustained a most wonderful marriage to the person who is, without any doubt, my soul mate. Everything I do is for her. That's a given.

But, this is different. This book is a labor of love and very special to me. Again, it has been a part of my life for a very long time and now, as I release it to the rest of you, I need to know who in my life would appreciate this the most. Who would have been smart enough, perceptive enough to understand exactly what I am trying to do? Who would have inspired me to go forward during those periods when I thought this would never end and I would never finish? I know he would have encouraged me to keep writing and he would have been sure that I would write what would be, to him at least, a masterpiece.

This book is dedicated to Theo; a man who I loved as if he were my own father. One who told me that he did, in fact, have *"my father's proxy in his hip pocket."* Nobody who ever knew me had more confidence in what I could do or who I was. He would never let me fail or even think about it. He was not my hero. He was more than that to me, but I believe I was his hero in many ways.

In the very short time that I knew Theo, he instilled a pride in me that will last forever. I know that Theo would be very proud of me today as I am and after what I have done. He would have been there all along by my side to help me in any way he could; emotionally or otherwise.

And so, have a chuckle or two on me because this is for you, Theo.

TABLE OF CONTENTS

WHO IS THIS GUY??

Right from the start, let me tell you that I do not have a PHD, I don't have a MBA, nor do I have a degree in Marketing from Harvard Business School (or any other school, for that matter). On the contrary, I'm the guy who dropped out of college to go sell something. I wanted the "buck" more than the degree. Right or wrong, that's the road I chose and it has served me well.

Now, don't get me wrong, I am not advocating the "DROP OUT" approach. Frankly, the one thing that I wish I had is that parchment paper that says I graduated, if for no other reason than having another feather for my cap. I am simply trying to identify myself as the proverbial "Peddler," which is a term that my wife hates. She cringes when I use it, but I love the term because the "Peddler" is the one that can stand toe-to-toe any day of the week with the most professional professionals.

To me, there are salesmen (excuse me, salespeople) and there are peddlers. There is a distinct difference and as we get into this writing, you'll more clearly see what I mean. But for now, suffice it to say that I hold the "Peddler" in very high regard. He is the consummate salesman, the great pitchman. If you understand what I mean, then you are the person to whom I am writing. Then again, maybe you need to see the PHD following the author's name. Believe me, there are plenty of those. However, quite honestly, I always had to wonder how all that formal education related to the gang warfare that the real salesperson encounters on the streets of the business world. This book is not for that guy (the one that needs to see the PHD) because that's not me at all.

I am, again, a college dropout who has made a career of sales and has made it big. I am not the CEO that could run General Motors, but I sure could sell the hell out of their cars. Then again, one of the greatest "Peddlers" ever was a guy named Iacocca who was called in to <u>sell</u> when all else failed. His sales ability, selling the world on Lee Iacocca, saved the company. Does Chrysler ring a bell?

So, now that you have the picture (if you don't, this book will not be for you), let me tell you why I'm doing this. I've always loved to write and I have reached a crossroads in my life and my career. Maybe it's time to take a deep breath and spend some time, one on one, with myself, putting some things down on paper. Who knows how far this will go? After all, this is not peddling, and, if something comes up that needs to be sold, I may need to take a break and go sell it. That's what I do. For now though, let's go on with this crossroads in my life and see if we can find a "Peddler" or two that needs some advice.

By the way, as you read the next part, understand that I am not feeling sorry for myself. Remember <u>Rule Number 1:</u> Never feel sorry for a real salesman because peddlers are not down for long, and if they find self pity, they weren't really peddlers in the first place.

Now that I've set the table, let's see what's on my plate.

FOREWORD/INTRODUCTION

Everyone will reach it one day, some sooner than others. For me, I'm about to turn 50 years old and it's a number I seem to hate more every day. For some reason I didn't mind 30, 35, 40, or even 45. I was one of those that had these canned answers when somebody asked me how it felt to be a certain age. I would say such things as, *"What's the alternative," "I feel better now than I've ever felt in my life," or "I wouldn't trade this place in my life for anything."*

This is different, however, and as I approach my 50th birthday (which is in a very few short weeks), I'm doing an awful lot of reflecting on what I've done with my life. Frankly, I feel old, and yes, I know that those people that I love so dearly that are in their 60s and 70s will tell me I'm just a kid and that my life is just beginning. But, somehow, I'm having a real tough time thinking youthfully. Then again, it may have something to do with the fact that my wife (who just happens to be 15 years my junior) made a comment the other day. She thought about me because she heard an ad on the radio that said I was now eligible for the Senior Games in St. George, Utah. This place is the ultimate retirement mecca to many people. That went over like the proverbial ton of bricks. I laughed right along with her and made light of her comment, but believe me, it hurt! In reality though, I guess I am eligible for the St. George Senior Games.

So, I'm doing all of this reflecting while I'm turning 50. I'm reaching another crossroads in my life because my biggest account, one that amounts to millions of dollars in sales and income, has just been sold and I need to make a decision. This decision has many factors to it. One factor is whether I want to follow this account to the other side of the world, better known as Arkansas, and try to continue selling or make a decision as to what I want to do with the rest of my life. I'm in anything but a desperate position and luckily I have the luxury that many people don't have when faced with this type of crisis. I don't have to go to work and I don't have to worry, at least for a while. Still, I'm a bit depressed because a couple more years of sustaining the business I was doing with this account would have provided me with a retirement of unquestionable status and luxury and the ability to do anything I really wanted to do. However, As I found out long ago, nothing is for sure and nothing is forever in the world of sales. We need to take the good (and there's lots of it) with the bad (and there's plenty of that). In many ways, I feel like someone who has been fired, and that's a terrible feeling. Actually, I've never had it before and now I know how someone feels who suffers the experience of going home and first telling the family they're out of work, and second, looking in the mirror and realizing it themselves.

One of the things that I would really like to do is to teach salespeople that are just starting out and help them to eliminate some of the mistakes that we all make. So, I decided that maybe the thing to do is to write this book and try to get it published. Frankly, at this point, I have no idea how to accomplish that. I guess the ultimate success (or failure) of this task will be determined if I figure it all out. I want to make it as simple as possible and to do it my way because, let's face it, that's the only way I know.

First, before I get into some of the things I want to talk about, let me briefly identify who I am and what I've done with my life so that maybe I can add a little credibility to what I'm writing here. I've often wondered, while reading numerous publications about sales, self-motivation, and so forth, if the person writing the piece really knew what they were talking about. Were they simply pontificating or were they experienced and capable of talking about some of these things? I always felt that it would be a real crime to mislead somebody that way. Therefore, for openers, it would be prudent for me to make sure I explained myself, listed my objectives, and identified who I am…………..

I've been a salesman in one way or another for 40 years. That's all I've ever done with my life, and proudly, I have always been successful. Sure, I've had my ups and I've had my downs. I've had my successes and I've had my failures, but in the long haul, I've made a lot of money (the reward for the downs)! I've been responsible for hundreds of millions of dollars in sales and dozens of employees. I had companies of my own where I personally wrote millions of dollars in business. I guess you could say that because of it all, for the most part, I've lived the good life. I'm relatively secure today, and proudly, I'm self-made. My professional career has spanned from that of being a young salesman, working for a company servicing stores, to that of a National Sales Manager of a major corporation. I have acted as consultant for a well-known licensee and spent the last part of my career as a Manufacturer's Sales Representative, which is what I currently do.

Today, in spite of the fact that my largest account has been sold, I own a firm that is one of the most successful and most respected Rep Agencies in the country. So, I think I'm qualified to write this book. I've done and seen many things and I know that people starting out make many mistakes. Perhaps this book will fulfill my objective of helping a few guys or a few gals through the infancy stages of being a salesperson. If I do that, I've accomplished my goal. Who knows, maybe I've decided what I want to do with the rest of my life.

Note: *This is being written at the beginning of this book. Again, it has taken ten years to write and the last part of the book, the last ten years, will be covered later.*

SO, YOU WANT TO BE A SALESPERSON!

For the most part, most people think that sales is easy. Everyone thinks that "if all else fails," they can always go and sell something. <u>WRONG, WRONG--EMPHATICALLY WRONG</u>! Get rid of that perception right now. It is simply a bunch of bull. Sales is not for everyone. "REAL" sales is a specialized field and the success rate is very low. Now, that does not take into consideration the clerk at a local department store or even the average car salesman. These people, although they are in actuality selling <u>something</u>, are not really salespeople. Sure, they would debate the issue and I understand their point of view (maybe), but I am writing this from my perspective. Although I've tried, I have a hard time calling a clerk a salesperson. Even the person that has a so-called "sales" job at a furniture store is not a professional, by any means. As I was discussing with my wife, just the other day, the furniture guy or gal is more of a clerk. "When is the last time a furniture salesperson actually sold you something"? Usually, you go to the store, walk around by yourself, even though you approached a time or two (or six) by some guy holding a book, catalogue or a clip board. Why? Who knows but its there. Wonder if he or she ever opens it up. Then, if you find a chair or something, the salesperson lets you know if its in stock or what colors it comes in. And, my friends, that's supposed to be sales! Who sold who what? The last thing I want to do is insult anyone. Therefore, I will take another moment or two to explain that I have, in fact, met and dealt with plenty of great, professional car salesmen. Let's face it though, these guys are few and very far between. In fact, later in the book, I talk about an exceptional fella who runs a car agency. This guy is the true exception. The truly prepared, product-educated car guy is a pleasure to deal with, but for the most part, they are high pressure and quite offensive. By the way, this is not to say that a bit of pressure is totally wrong. Hey, I've been known to choke the old juggler myself from time to time. But the fine line is to know when to stop and knowing what you're doing. The "quite offensive" part happens when the pressure is put on by someone who has no idea what is going on or what he or she is talking about. Sounds like the average car guy to me! Besides, to my way of thinking, anyone who waits around all day for the customer to show up is not really a salesman anyway. Maybe as I proceed, you'll get a clearer perspective of what I am trying to say. Remember though, this is very important, at least to me. It is about perception and if that concept is not totally in line, you simply cannot proceed with this type of career. A salesperson CREATES. He or she does not wait for something to happen. Believe me, I've seen far too many talented people fail in this game because they did not understand who they really were. At the expense of being redundant, this is not for everyone. I'm going to spend a little more time on this matter. We need to see ourselves as others see us before we can truly develop the *"I DON'T CARE ATTITUDE"* that is essential to and goes with great sales success.

THE PRETENDERS AND THE ENEMY............

They know that ...*we are a hustling bunch of lies, all wrapped up in a human, smooth-talking body.*

I've already talked about the perception that many have about how easy it is to sell. I've also identified some who think they are salespeople, but to me (and in all actuality), they are not. Let's continue on that thought and look further into those that I call "THE PRETENDERS." The other day I stopped at the local 7-Eleven, as I do every morning for a cup of coffee, and heard the clerk mention to a customer that he had "sold" four donuts that morning. What a guy, I thought. So early in the morning and this guy had already made some sales, and chocolate donuts to boot. It must have been tough! (SERVING DONUTS IS NOT SALES)

Of course, you know I'm being sarcastic, but the statement merely pointed out something that irks my professional pride. The term *sale*, along with the reference to *salesman* (or salesperson) is used too often and much too often. How in the world can we get the respect we deserve as peddlers (here I go again) if the guy at 7Eleven thinks he actually "sold" some donuts? A figure of speech, you say? Perhaps, but it is something to help me to prove a point. You see, there is and has to be a clear and distinct definition of what a real salesperson is. He or she is not, absolutely not, a clerk at the local convenience store. Now don't get me wrong. There is nothing wrong with working at the local convenience store. It is, undoubtedly, an honorable job (boy, am I being generous) and a worthy profession for anyone who chooses to do it, but it is not sales in any way, shape, or form. Neither is the task of manning the drive-through window at McDonalds and telling me, "It's the second yogurt or the fifth Big Mac I sold today."

Let me add here that at another point in this book, I will talk in depth about the clerk and point out the fact that I do, in many ways, respect them. I really do! I want to discuss how they should be perceived and how they are not. In other words, they do have their place, even in this book. There is plenty of pride and credibility here, but not to this particular point that I am trying to make. Don't close the cover yet if you are a bank teller (etc.). I'll get to you later. Back to my friend at McDonald's. Buddy, you did not sell me a yogurt and the 7-Eleven guy did not sell any donuts. You both served the little goodies only after they were either picked up or ordered ahead of time. Serving donuts is serving donuts. Its not Sales! I even wrote a book about it.

Now sit back, close your eyes, and think of all the times someone told you that they sold something, when in fact, they did anything but. If you still can't see it, then this is not your deal, believe me! Close the cover now. Its OK! I'm not being arrogant or rude, but the fact really is that sales is a profession to those of us who have fought all the battles for so long in the "SALES JUNGLE." It smarts just a bit to hear the gal at the local theater talking about "selling" (cringe time for me, every week) popcorn to someone who has spent the last week putting together a professional proposal that could generate millions of dollars in revenue for a customer.

LET'S CALL THESE GUYS AND GALS PRETENDERS!

The very first thing you need to do is to clearly identify what and who constitutes a salesperson. Remember, it is not what others think of you or how they perceive you. Unfortunately, we will always be misunderstood. It is how we feel about ourselves and how we look at each other. Someone who dedicates his or her life to sales and succeeds is a professional. That person should be as respected as any lawyer, doctor, or other professional.

Above, I mentioned that we would always be misunderstood. Maybe I should expound on that just a bit. After all, it is a strong statement, but, as you will learn day by day in this business, it is quite true. Ask the average person (if there is such a thing) what he perceives as a salesman.

Years ago there was a TV sitcom called *WKRP in Cincinnati*. Most of you, I will assume, are much too young to remember this show and that's unfortunate. It was about a radio station and the characters were the personnel that worked at it. There was a character in the show, the salesman, whom to this day, I fear we are still compared to. This guy walked around in plaid red and green pants, yellow sport coat, striped shirt, and a paisley tie. Those of us who remember the show will never forget that "dude." Those of you who are too young, well, just try to let your imagination run. This guy was truly a piece of work. It had to say something about our perception if they created that character to look like that, didn't it? He was a nice enough guy, but sadly, not very bright (then again, we're all uneducated, you know), pretty obnoxious, and above all else, poor as a church mouse. Get

5

it? He was the salesman but not at all successful. All the poor slob wanted was a date with a gorgeous, voluptuous actress named Loni Anderson (all salesmen are philanderers too, you know), but it was a constant exercise in frustration. The object of the whole thing was clear. This guy was a loser, anything but successful and he was the salesman. What a perception! What about Danny DeVito in another great movie, *The Tin Man*? Which, I must add, is one of my all-time favorite movies and one that every salesperson, old or new, must see. In fact, I used to insist on it with those who worked for me. Probing questions followed. In fact, you should all see the movie and then try to figure out the message in it. If you're a true peddler, you will. It was a movie built around a bunch of high rollers who spent their entire lives cheating everyone. In the end, they all failed, all went bust, and all remained the proverbial scumbags. Another great perception that we all have to answer to.

Then there was Al Pacino and Jack Lemmon in *Glengarry Glen Ross*. Again, the typical insinuations of the lowlifes we are all supposed to be, but another great movie and one that you really ought to see. I could go on and on. I've mentioned all this because I need you to know that this is how you are perceived. I don't care what anyone says, either to your face or behind your back, our chosen profession is the most misunderstood and most stereotyped occupation. It's like saying that all doctors are millionaires and all lawyers are crooks. To the average person, they feel that way about doctors and lawyers, and they know that *we are a hustling bunch of lies all wrapped up in a human, smooth-talking body.* By the way, I love that definition. I wonder how many people would love to have thought that one up when trying to describe all of us. Now that we've met the Pretenders, how about identifying the enemy? This may surprise you, but if you think the average person has misconceptions of us, wait until you meet the buyer who will be your customer.

Put the buyer in his or her proper place right now! He or she is not and never will be your friend or your neighbor. In fact, the longer I spend in this business, the more I realize the truth. The person with the pen is anything but your friend. Go fishing with someone else!

THE ENEMY...

While I'm painting the picture, let me go a little further. I might as well get it all out of the way before I turn the tables and prove to you that they are all wrong. I need to take a moment and talk about the buyers that you will meet as you go through "the jungle."

Here's my NUMBER ONE BUYER RULE:

Remember, no buyer that you will ever meet or do any business with will ever make as much money as you do and he or she will know it! Regardless of how you come off, low-key or high-key, you will never convince a buyer that you are not at least ten times richer than you are.

NUMBER TWO BUYER RULE:

You will never convince a buyer that you have earned any part of your success. Every ONE will contend to his or her dying day that everything you have, everything you've done, is pure luck, plain and simple.

And here is my NUMBER THREE BUYER RULE:

Always remember, taking Rule 1 and Rule 2 into account, every buyer will be totally convinced that you owe him everything and you are responsible for him and his family.

And ... NUMBER FOUR BUYER RULE:

Again, taking all the above into consideration, never build yourself up for a letdown by expecting any buyer to pay for anything in your presence. Forget it! It is not going to happen! This rule states that if you're out with a buyer, alone or with his spouse, it is going to be your deal 100%. In 30 years, I have received one Coke from one guy and he has never let me forget it. That Coke was bought at an NBA Playoff game in Chicago where I spent more than $1,000.00 for tickets and bought dinner to boot.

What does all this have to do with wanting to be a salesperson, you ask. This picture needs to be painted to put this profession in its proper perspective. By better understanding the negative side (sides), you'll have more fun enjoying the positive side, which is a chance to make lots of bucks. Just remember, you are not in this deal to make friends, especially with the buyers.

While I am on the subject of buyers, let me paint another little sketch on the canvas. We're talking about how buyers perceive us. Remember that not one buyer you will ever meet will make anywhere near as much money as you, and knowing that, regardless of what you think, he will resent you. Try to come to grips with the revelation that you will be treated like garbage much of the time! It will become the buyer or merchant's turn, in his or her way, to punish you for having the courage to do something with your life that requires self-discipline and the self-guided direction to determine success.

I clearly remember, very early in my career, a very prominent motivational lecturer referring to the buyer as a "SMALL-TIME CHARLIE WHO WILL ALWAYS BE A SMALL-TIME CHARLIE." He went on to say, "THE ONLY CHANCE THAT SMALL-TIME CHARLIE EVER HAS TO BE BIG-TIME IS WHEN HE TAKES THE SALESMAN, YOU, TO THE MAT." Although I have tried throughout my career to think otherwise, I am afraid that for the most part, this is completely correct. It will now be in your best interest to make sure this is understood and is in the back of your mind throughout your career.

So now, with this picture of the customer who will control your destiny, what is our task to overcome this feeling of apparent distaste for our profession? For now, let's make it simple and let me try to paint another picture. Perhaps I should be a painter, not an author! Anyway, try to picture the buyer as seeing you, the salesperson, walking into his or her office as "the enemy." Strange as that may seem, they really do see us that way. Anyway, let's pretend that he or she sees himself or herself as a poor soul, hanging over the edge of a cliff by his or her fingernails, barely hanging on. He sees you, Mr. Salesperson, as some well-dressed dude walking over to the cliff and stepping on his hand, crushing his fingers and making him loose grip. Guess what's next? Our job and eternal goal is to change that buyer's image of us and try to get him to feel that instead of stepping on his fingers, we are reaching down and pulling him up. You are not going to hurt the poor fella (or gal), but instead, save him (or her). Try to remember this little scene as you interact with the customer.

Let me give you one more example. Many years ago, when I was just beginning, I had an item that I thought was pretty great. I since learned that all of my products, at least as I felt about them, were pretty great. In fact, there were many times that I thought the world's shittiest product was great! Anyway, in this particular case, I was living in Southern California and took it to the local department store. After presenting the item to the buyer, he suggested that I present it to his boss, The Merchandise Manager. The buyer arranged for the appointment and escorted me into the manager's office. He was an elderly gent, a bit worn, but looking very accomplished behind his desk. I need to note that at that point in my sales career, anyone sitting behind a desk, in a suit, being called a Merchandise manager, would have been impressive (maybe intimidating is a better word) to me. After a minute or two of small talk and just when I was about to make my presentation, he asked the young buyer to leave the office, leaving me alone with him. Now, remember, I was just beginning and now I'm alone with this guy. He then set the stage for my lifelong feelings toward buyers and the formation of my "CLIFF" story as told above.

HE GAVE ME "THE RULES."

I knew right then that sales was a thankless job and my only reward would be the good life, but one that I would have to earn by eating crow. I was willing to settle for that. He said something to the effect that it really didn't matter what I had to sell because, after all, it was my item and he didn't know anywhere near what I knew about it. If I believed in it, then we would be able to sell it to them, but only under his rules and with the following understanding. He said, "Save the sales pitch, young man. I've heard them all. We'll buy the damn thing and if it sells, then I'm a hero. If it bombs, then you bomb with it and take it back." In other words, he wins either way and all I get is the commission and no glory. He went on to say that I might as well understand early on that "this is how it works." Well, he was right and I have never forgotten his little lesson. By the way, the item went in, sold quite well, and Mr. Merchandise Manager was a hero. Nobody really ever cared (or knew) who the sales guy was; however, I went on to sell the account for many years and made lots of dollars, all the while making sure that I followed the rules and made our manager a hero. So be it!

Now that you've decided you want to be a salesperson and you know who you are going to sell, let's really identify who you are, because, my friends, you are not The Tin Man, the guy on WKRP, or the dried-up, old peddler from *Glengarry Glen Ross*. On the contrary, you are a fabulous, well-groomed professional who has chosen a life of pride and accomplishment. You have guts and the ability to take on any obstacle that you face and the confidence to succeed. You are everything other than what these perceptions show you as.

Let's find out who you are...

WHAT IS A PEDDLER AND WHAT DOES HE DO?

I'm always surprised at how little the average person knows about sales. As we discussed before, perception of the entire field is often misunderstood. We've already determined how others look at us, but here I want to explore how people view sales as a whole.

Out of curiosity, ask almost anyone how they think merchandise gets to the shelves of the local K-Mart, or for that matter, any store. The average person has no idea what a Sales Representative is. They cannot understand, until it is explained to them, that every single item that is sold must have exposure to some salesperson before it is actually passed on to a buyer. How many hands does a small product touch before it is sold?

These things are taken for granted and never realized until pointed out. Then again, who really cares?

On the many occasions that I had the opportunity to interview prospective employees, I always found it interesting that rarely did anyone realize what a Sales Rep did. Sure, they thought they knew, but in reality, they had no idea. Even more peculiar were those who wanted to join us for a job in sales but really knew nothing about it. I could understand the administrative applicant, but not, the sales recruit?

Then again, I guess I can understand because of all the misguided information that goes along with the misconceptions that abound. As a point of reference, the other day I picked up a "so-called" sales book that was written by a PhD (who else). You already know my thoughts on that subject, but anyway,

I opened a random page. What do you think I read by this "expert" on sales?

He gave his firm opinion that ALL PEOPLE, EVERYONE, IS A SALESPERSON IN ONE WAY OR THE OTHER. Right there, he lost all credibility in my eyes. Does that mean the 7-Eleven "donut" clerk is a salesman, and perhaps, my thoughts as previously expressed are arguable? It's ridiculous to think that all people are in sales. To him, convincing children to eat their spinach is a sales job of sorts and so on. That direction is the basis for writing a book, but it is not my direction, my basis, or my philosophy. WE ARE NOT ALL SALESPEOPLE, PLAIN AND SIMPLE!! If I accomplish nothing more than to instill big-time pride in the people who are serious about sales as a career who read this book, then I will be happy.

Webster describes SALESPERSON as ... *A person employed to sell goods*. That's simple enough, and for the most part, it's true, but I cannot let this thing be too simple. Remember, I'm talking about (and to) the people who want to be peddlers, and Webster describes a peddler as ... *A person that goes from place to place selling*.

There is the difference, as clearly put as a basic set of definitions in Webster's dictionary. He or she does not have the luxury of having the customer come to him.

So, who are we talking about? Think of all the types of salespeople that peddle. It's everything from the insurance agent to the gal that sold my kids a World Book set several weeks ago.From the soft-water guy to the siding salesperson (Tin Man). Then there are the people who are called "REPS," or more distinctly, Sales Representatives. For the most part, these are the guys and gals I'm talking to because, in all fairness, this is what I do and have done most of my professional career. I am, as they say, A REP! So, while I will be speaking from a Rep's point of view, I trust everything I say and every contention I make will apply to all salespeople that derive income from pursuing and developing business away from the office. That would include the typical "DOOR TO DOOR" salesperson (World Books, softeners, etc.) as well as The Rep. There are basically two types of Reps. I'm not going to get into much detail now because it is a subject that I will discuss in depth extensively later on. After all, when all the smoke clears and I get down to business, I hope to help some of you become Reps or be better ones than you are. This book is for you. So, let me take just a moment to define the two basic types of Reps and go on. By the way, so far it's been all smoke and I see no sign of it clearing for a few more pages anyway. Outside salespeople can either work for a company or be independent. These are the two basic differences. Let's say, as an example, that a major manufacturer elects to go to market by using their own salespeople. They would hire Representatives to call on their accounts for them. These people will be exclusive, selling only those products brought to market by that one manufacturer. This Rep is usually treated as an employee by receiving certain benefits such as insurance, cars or allowances, expenses, retirement, and so on. It's usually a good job and can evolve into areas of Sales Management where, for the most part, the benefits improve, as does the money. As an example, I started my sales career as a salesman, working for a large company in the stationery industry, calling on small independent stores. I worked on a small salary basis. I grew with that company, advancing to several management positions including District

Manager, Regional Manager, and finally, National Sales Manager before deciding to pursue my own sales company.

That brings me to the second type of Rep, the independent. This is the real peddler because the INDEPENDENT MANUFACTURER'S SALES REP is playing for all the marbles without any crutch at all. Success is entirely in his or her hands. This person takes advantage of the manufacturer that elects not to employ his or her own salespeople. Instead, they decide to hire independents on a straight-commission basis.

In many respects, this is a much less expensive route to take since sales costs are a minimum of what the expenses really are. There are no "BENNIES" or benefits. The independent pays his or her own taxes, expenses, and transportation. There is a fee paid for sales and that's it. There are advantages and disadvantages to both situations. The company pays a great deal more for the in-house person. He or she is their salesperson exclusively. They carry only what that particular company brings to market. The downside is that this person is much more expensive and the company assumes greater responsibility. At the same time, there is ownership, if I can be so blunt! The independent is much less expensive, and for the most part, usually better connected at the customer level. I say that because this person is one who usually has been around longer and has the important contacts that most manufacturers desire.

The manufacturer needs to weigh this against the fact that, as an independent, the company has less control. The Rep in this case can carry several lines (non-competing) and thus does not devote 100% of his or her attention to a given manufacturer. This person is usually referred to as a

Manufacturer's Representative, and this guy, for all intents and purposes, is the peddler that makes the most bucks. He is also the guy that takes the biggest risk, but, as we will learn, risk comes with reward. We'll be addressing the Independent Sales Rep often in this book.

Earlier, I suggested that the average person has no real idea of what a salesperson does or how goods get to market. Now that we have defined and simplified the definition of Salesperson and Peddler, we need to remember that the people we speak to who are not related to our business generally are not clued in to what it takes to get goods on the shelf. Do not be guilty of taking anyone for granted. If you do, we will never stop the misconceptions about us. Ask the question and be prepared to give the answer.

We are the proverbial "Middlemen." Walk through any store, any aisle, and whatever you see was put there by a salesperson. I don't care what it is. Nothing, absolutely nothing goes on a sales floor without some salesperson selling it. The goods that are for sale, the fixtures that hold them, the carpet we walk on, the registers that take our money, were all sold by someone. The salesperson has received a fee for everything we see. Going further, open the hood of your car and count the parts. Every one of those plugs, wires, nuts, and bolts were sold by someone and somebody was paid to sell it.

As you can see, we are important guys and gals, aren't we? This stuff is pretty basic and simple. As I said earlier, I will get into more depth later, but for now, I think we have defined a few things and we can now go on.

DISCIPLINE, DISCIPLINE, DISCIPLINE

……..Plan your work and work your plan!

In real estate, agents often use the expression "LOCATION, LOCATION, LOCATION" to describe a prime property. It is, as they will often eagerly explain, the sole most important factor in buying real estate. If the location is correct, everything else falls into place.

In sales, especially outside sales as we have been defining, it is DISCIPLINE, DISCIPLINE, DISCIPLINE that will ultimately be the difference between success and failure. There is simply no one ingredient that means more. The lack of discipline will cause failure <u>every time</u>. It never fails. If a person does not have the regulation, organization, and order that go hand–in–hand with discipline, he or she will undoubtedly find sales to be a confusing, chaotic, disorderly, frustrating mess. I have seen so many people through the years that had so very much talent, but because of the lack of discipline, wasted their time trying to sell.

Sales is much more than simply presenting something. Certainly, that in and of itself is important. At some point in this book, we will dissect the sale and look at the presentation as a separate subject. Here though, I am talking about something much more important than the actual presentation of wares. As I mentioned before, I have seen so many "great" pitchmen blow a sales career because they lacked the perseverance that goes with the job.

At a very young age, I had a boss that overused the expression, "PLAN YOUR WORK – WORK YOUR PLAN." He would advise us to tape it to our foreheads (he actually did it to some of us) and keep it in mind constantly. For a while, I would find myself repeating the phrase for what seemed to be constantly every day. Frankly, it drove me nuts! I knew for sure that whenever I had occasion to walk into his office, before too long he would find a reason to say, "Klein, remember, plan your work and work your plan." Yes sir, yes sir, and yes sir! It drove me whacko. You know something, I have never forgotten it, and I must admit, I have probably repeated that little phrase 20,000 times to others in my lifetime. There is simply no other set of words that says it quite like, *"PLAN YOUR WORK AND WORK YOUR PLAN."*

If you think about it, nothing is done <u>correctly</u> unless it is planned out carefully. You will build a home only after plans are drawn and followed precisely. Try deviating from home plans and I assure you, there will surely be a crooked wall somewhere. Professional athletes spend hours practicing and planning for games or matches. Afterward, they will always refer to the term "execution" when discussing and describing success or failure. Either they executed properly or they did not execute at all. What was executed? Their game plan! It is the meter that judges winning and losing, and it only works with discipline in working the plan.

By now, you are (or should be) thinking about all the things that require plans in order to succeed. It is almost endless. The same principles of planning and execution apply to sales and the career of selling.

Today's business environment demands, more and more, the use of computers. Many of the programs are designed to help organize businesspeople. They create the ability to plan days, weeks, months, and even years. They teach us to follow through and follow up. They offer us "TO DO" lists that help us update what we need to accomplish daily. Itineraries are established and organized. All this with one thing and only one thing in mind. You can take computers with you and organize as you go, in your car, in the park, in the restaurant. There simply is no excuse today. The effort level is so much lower in today's environment.

These programs are designed to keep us organized so that we can adequately plan our work. In today's business environment, it is essential that schedules are established and confirmed well in advance. Because it has become so expensive to travel, we need to make certain our organizational skills are in order. We need to plan!

Now that we have figured out a way to plan, we need to understand that we are now only halfway there. We now need to work that plan, and, folks, this

is where discipline, discipline, discipline comes in. I have known so many through the years who were very able to get to the point of total and complete organization. They would spend all these hours planning and then could not figure out what to do with the plan. Taking the next step, we need to work the plan that we have worked on, and that is called EXECUTION. In another chapter in this book, I speak about winning and football, specifically Joe Gibbs. His bottom line, as is the bottom line of all great coaches, is also execution.

To execute properly, you have to be smart. The more successful salesperson is the smarter person, especially as it relates to what we are talking about here.

Salespeople have to get up every day and start over. We need to look at each new day as a new experience and challenge. Forget the failures of the past week or so. It's time to start over when that alarm goes off. If we visit an account and are treated shabbily and rudely (and you sure will - bet on it), we need to find it in ourselves to forget it immediately and go on to the next guy with a positive attitude. That, even I will admit, is tough. When I first started out, I would make ten cold calls (no appointments) a day. Because of the nature of the particular business, I failed a large percentage of the time (I hate like hell to admit that, even now). That is, until I figured it all out and drastically changed the percentages. Anyway, after each negative, I would slap myself in the face and start again. I mean it; I would actually slap myself. By the end of some days, I was a bit bruised. It worked though, and I was able to wake myself up each time and go on in a positive way. I'm not suggesting you beat yourself to a pulp, but it's a little trick that worked for me. Maybe you need to try a little pinch, some cold water, or better yet, find something that sells well and enjoy a high success rate.

The point is that we cannot dwell on the past. This applies to good or bad events. Every day, every call is new and different. It must be handled that way, and to do so, we need to develop discipline. To succeed, we must be dedicated, have a great degree of perseverance, drive, and above all else, the guts to stick it out!

TWO EARS AND ONE MOUTH ...

When most of us think about salespeople, we envision a smooth-talking, very aggressive person that is doing most, if not all, of the talking. Certainly, salespeople talk a great deal. I will be the first to admit that the great peddler wants nothing more than to dominate the conversation. In fact, many of us live in fear that all will be lost if someone else takes over. This is especially true when referring to sales presentations because, as we all know, the peddler seems to live and die with the success or failure of every brand-new sales pitch. It is as if the entire perpetuation of a career is weighing heavily on the moment. So, the appearance of intensity is certainly well-founded, and that's why we seem to envision some of these guys wringing their sweaty hands in anticipation of the pending presentation. So many times, I have amused myself by sitting in the lobby of a buying office, watching a member of the sales community looking much like a prize fighter warming up in his corner before the bell sounds.

Looking like the expectant father, this guy is pacing the floor, waiting for the buyer (who is, I need to add, usually late, which only makes the poor pacer more nervous). Although I never witnessed this myself, I would be willing to bet that many a fine young salesperson, overwhelmed with nerves, was carried out of a buying office on a stretcher, oxygen mask in place and I.V. bottle hanging at his side. What a sight! Well, perhaps I'm being a bit dramatic, (WHO ME?) but again, I wouldn't be at all surprised.

I often wondered what the customer would think if he happened to see this spectacle. Does he think this salesperson is acting like the world is balancing on this moment, across the desk from some merchant? No wonder the buyers treat us with such disdain and contempt. Remember the "SMALL-TIME CHARLIE" scenario or the picture of the poor slob "HANGING BY HIS FINGERNAILS?" Here we are, representing major companies who have put all this trust in us, acting like punch-drunk palookas waiting for the sales bell to ring. Consequently, there are many who, when they finally get in the sales ring, talk so much that they blow the entire opportunity. This is one of the reasons, as stated before, most new salespeople fail. In short, they talk too damn much, plain and simple! They get so nervous and excited about the chance to make a pitch that they don't take the time to find out what the hell the customer may or may not need. Instead, they jabber themselves into oblivion. As I look back at my early days in sales management when I spent a great amount of time making calls with new people, the most frustrating thing (and hardest thing to break) was watching these kids blow it by talking too much. The situation could rarely be corrected because, no matter how hard we managers would try to correct the overzealousness (too much blabbing), the salesperson wouldn't hear what we had to say. You know why? He was talking too much, defending himself, and he couldn't hear what I was trying to teach. In every case, when terminated for not making the grade, the inevitable question would be, "BUT WHY?" and the stock answer was always, "BECAUSE YOU DIDN'T LISTEN."

To be successful in sales, you need to learn to listen. When I was a very young boy, my father would get frustrated when trying to tell me something because I was doing too much talking. He would say, "GOD GAVE US TWO EARS AND ONE

MOUTH BECAUSE HE WANTED US TO LISTEN TWICE AS MUCH AS WE TALKED." He was so right, and you know, that little statement, remembering "POP" saying it, quite frankly saved many sales for me because it made me shut up. In fact, I remember many times when I found myself overblabbing in a presentation and I could sense the buyer getting tired of it all. I would actually stop myself, hopefully in time to save the deal but not always. I not only subscribed to the saying but I have used it over and over again in my career. I am emphatically making a point of it now and urging each and every one of you to remember it as I have because IT IS TRUE. Let the customer talk. He or she will ultimately let you in on the little secret that will always get you the sale. He or she will give you the answers to what he or she wants, needs, or doesn't need. The buyer will tell you their objections so that you can be prepared to answer. If you do all the talking, you will hear nothing, and usually get nothing. Again, listen twice as much as you talk. The buyer is expecting you to run wild at the mouth. When you don't and you listen to him instead, he is surprised and relieved to have found someone eager to reach down and pick him up off the edge of the cliff. I keep getting back to that, but the more graphic I get, the more you might remember the little things that stick out and create success.

When we're young and new at this game, we seem to panic. Panic makes us talk and not listen, and so, the young guys often find the road frustrating. As we get older and more experienced, we become less panicked and we tend to take more time. That's called experience and with it comes patience and, yes, smoothness. That's the term I hear so often when a young salesperson witnesses an old pro making a pitch. I need to add, would be remiss if I didn't, that some Sales Managers should not be Sales Managers because they talk too damn much. I am not speaking of the good ones here. Usually the new guy is awestruck and cannot help but to describe the event and the "Pro" as SMOOTH. Perhaps what he really means is that the guy was not in a rush. He has learned to be patient, to listen, and to absorb the moment while trying to ascertain what the buyer needs and wants. He is able to control the presentation. That should be why he or she is in management. By listening, I have learned that the customer will often lead us right to the correct button that opens the cash register. So remember, "TWO EARS AND ONE MOUTH SO WE CAN LISTEN TWICE AS MUCH AS WE TALK"--Good advice from a great advisor. Thanks, Dad!

TAKING AN INVENTORY!

A great many things can happen to someone that becomes successful in sales. It goes without saying that we do this for the money. We have heard of people that do in fact follow and pursue careers for other reasons. Some simply are not motivated by the dollar, but in the case of sales, I feel justified and quite comfortable in making the general statement that money is <u>THE</u> motivator in this business. The glory that comes with our success, the badge on our lapels (if you will), the proverbial gold watch, is the money we earn, and in most cases, we earn lots. Some people save lives, others defend lives, many teach, but let's face it, the salesperson makes money, not glory. The salesperson, one that has been around a long time and especially the so-called "REP" as we've been describing, is usually very successful and earns lots of it. The fact is that there have been times when the large amount of money earned has created serious problems, not only for the individual, his agency, or firm, but for entire industries. Customers, specifically buyers who don't earn very much, resent salespeople who seemingly earn a great deal. We've already talked about this and will touch on it from time to time as we proceed. Anyway, it is a daily stumbling block. It is our cross to bear, as they say.

Earlier, I mentioned an entire industry affected by the amount of money those of us in sales earn. Several years ago, those of us in the sales industry were shocked when we learned that one of the country's biggest retailers directed their employees to stop dealing with Independent Reps. In fact, why mince words? It was the world's largest retailer, Wal-Mart. In fact, the CEO of the retailer actually sent letters to every existing supplier asking that they eliminate their Reps and start calling on the account themselves. The account was, and is, so big that the manufacturers, for the most part, had no choice but to honor the request.

I was in the rep business at the time, and believe me, it infuriated us.

Needless to say, this created a great deal of havoc in the industry. First, from our point of view, how could a retailer dictate policy to the manufacturer and get away with it? I personally knew Reps that made literally millions of dollars each year by calling on the account, only to get wiped out overnight. Wal-Mart wanted the Rep gone and the commissions turned into discounts. It was a devastating blow to say the least. The fear was that this would give the account a big edge (3% or 5% is a huge advantage). Other retailers would have no choice but to do the same thing. Yet, regardless of a national uprising that included Class Action lawsuits, the customer basically prevailed. Today, few if any independents call on this major account. It is considered by most suppliers to be a "HOUSE ACCOUNT" and one that is called on by headquarters' people. The account was so big that the manufacturers had to comply. Does that mean they screwed the Reps, the very ones that got them the business in the first place? You be the judge. I personally never knew who I was more upset with, Mr. Wal-Mart or the factories that didn't have the guts to support us. There are many theories and tales told as to why the sudden change and decision to write such a new policy. After all, it is a fact that Reps called on the account successfully for many years, and admittedly, many were responsible for much of the account's incredible growth. Why then did this edict go out without any apparent notice? Again, there are many theories, and I've heard most, but after all the stories have been sorted out, evaluated, and analyzed, it all comes down to the amount of money the Reps were making. In fact, the prevailing theory is based on a story that goes like this. The founder of the account and one of the richest men in the world, Sam Walton, who looked like he didn't have a dime, was looking at property in Arkansas. He found a piece of land that happened to be on the river across from some extraordinarily beautiful homes. One home in particular caught his eye and he inquired about it. The realtor knew who owned the home and conveyed the information that the owner was, in fact, a Food Broker (REP) that made all his money selling to this gentleman's chain. For some reason, it was beyond comprehension to this billionaire that anyone in sales could generate that type of income. He became enraged for some strange reason, went back to his headquarters, inquired about this particular Rep, asked about several others, and for all intents and purposes, counted their money. He then made his feelings known that he would not tolerate this type of income being made by salespeople because he felt their commission would be better used on his bottom line. He believed that "Reps" were worthless and no longer needed. So the now-famous letter was sent out, and as we speak, The Rep as we know him or her is not welcome at this account. In fact, that single event probably changed the rep business as we knew it. The business, at least for me, changed, and it was then that I began thinking of doing something else. More about that later, though.

So, along with the opportunity to earn lots of money, we need to make sure that we realize the dangers that go with it.

It is so easy with success to begin taking things for granted. This is when I see the symptoms of what I call "THE DEADLY SALES DISEASE." To put it another way, this disease is called arrogance, and, my friends, it is easier to get in this business than the common cold. For every one of us, when we enjoy a degree of success, we will, without fail, suffer this disease. If it lasts too long, it can and often does destroy us. Of all the human failings that can destroy a business, arrogance is the deadliest. The problem is that it is very easy to get, but almost impossible to recognize. When we are successful, it is so easy to stop doing the "little things" that made us successful. We tend to let others do them, but our arrogance rubs off on the others around us and, thus, the proverbial "chip" on the shoulder is seen as ordinary throughout the entire organization. Arrogance is contagious, and if we have it ourselves, we cannot see it in others, and so we tolerate it.

To others, however, it sticks out like a wart on the end of your nose. To the arrogant one, he or she is so busy being successful that the wart goes unnoticed. Ask yourself if you like arrogant people. Neither does your customer.

Let's relate this to the Wal-Mart scenario. Every one of us wants to grow and become important to the "big" accounts. That's the nature of this business. We use the smaller accounts as stepping stones, so to speak, to get to the big ones. So, let's say these Reps called on all the little accounts for years and then they scored with Wal-Mart. Who needs the little guy anymore? You now have the big hitter and all the commission that goes with it. You're making the big bucks, living on the hill with the doctors, lawyers, and athletes. Well, that's all fine as long as Mr. Wal-Mart doesn't see some big piece of "Rep" property across the river. Those that were affected had to go back to their smaller accounts to survive. Some, at least those who were smart enough to maintain a good professional relationship throughout, were welcomed back and supported. Those that became arrogant and forgot who got them there in the first place began looking for a new career. Get it? Here's a very important rule (another one) that I have implemented throughout my career, regardless of the job I was doing. *I always tried to treat every account, customer, or buyer, regardless of their size, as if they were my biggest account. And quite frankly, for that moment, they were.*

No one is immune from this disease, which is so often the affliction of successful people. In fact, I was stricken at one point in my own career. Believe me, I had no idea how absolutely obnoxious I was becoming. Lucky for me, I have always been able to develop honest relationships (to whatever degree possible) with customers. One day, while walking through a buying office, I was stopped by a customer who asked if I had a moment to chat. Thinking it was an opportunity to sell something, I marched immediately into his office and sat down. Perhaps what happened that day might very well have changed my life and my career. It is, without any doubt, something that I have always remembered.

I was told that my attitude had changed and that I was acting "as if I owned the joint." I was being cocky and he felt he was doing me a favor by pointing it out. It was embarrassing while at the same time sobering. I left somewhat upset and spent the rest of the day looking in the mirror. What I saw, quite honestly, was someone whom I did not like at all. I was unknowingly inflicted with my own power and success. I had allowed it to get to my head, to affect my outward appearance and personality. Here I was, the guy that started with nothing, letting my success get the best of me. It was time to regroup, understand what happened, and go forward. I was, in many ways, very lucky to have had someone tell me what he had been seeing. I decided that day that I would take the time to remember where I came from, how I started out, and how difficult it was to get where I was. I call it *"taking an inventory."*

UP AND DOWN

I know for sure that any one of you who gets through this rather strange little book (at least I know it) will be successful. I have that much confidence in you. My fear is of what will happen after I'm long gone and the book has been thrown away or left somewhere.

So, my dear friends, it's time that I put a little warning in here, just in case. It could be the most important thing I have said so far. I know, I say that about everything, don't I? So, I'm enthusiastic. Cut me some slack. This reminds me of my dear wife who used to enjoy when I'd bring home new products and declare, *"Now this is the greatest item."* To this day, she teases me about all the "greatest" items I used to sell.

Getting back to this point (I tend to wander - forgive me), you need to understand the expression, "YOU MEET THE SAME PEOPLE ON THE WAY DOWN THAT YOU MET ON THE WAY UP." What an absolutely profound statement. Think about it. I actually heard it first as a very young man of 18 or so. I made friends with someone in the music industry and I had the chance to hang out at Capital Records for a few days. There was this big star, or at least he once was, a singer who had many hits, sold millions of records, and was considered one of the best entertainers in the world.

His name was Bobby Darren (Mack The Knife). I guess Bobby had one fault. He was a cocky, brash, rude young man who pissed lots of people off. When it so happened that his career began to stutter, he found little support in the industry. People hated the guy, and he had to fight his way back, on his own. Anyway, here I was at Capital one day, and Bobby comes walking through. He was actually quite nice to me, but a real jerk to my friend. I wanted to talk about it. That's when he told me the expression about meeting the same people on the way down, and Mr. Darren was, in fact, in the midst of free fall. He told me to picture it as a ladder. I guess as he was going up the ladder of success, this fabulous entertainer who had the world on a string forgot to say please, thanks, and all that good stuff. In other words, he was a jerk. People never forgot, and when he began to fall, he could get absolutely no help. The rungs of the ladder broke as he stepped on them. Bobby did in fact come back but never all the way. Certainly not to where he should have or could have been.

The lesson learned there was one that I have seen repeated many times through the years. It's usually a sad case of self-destruction. Just the other night, for example, I took my son to an NBA Basketball game here in Phoenix. All of a sudden, I saw Kareem Abdul Jabbar coming up the steps, heading right for us. I told my son that he was about to be in the presence of perhaps the greatest basketball player ever.

He was the most prolific scorer who ever played the game. He was also, as legend had it, the world's biggest asshole, to put it bluntly. Kareem spent a career scoring points, earning championship rings, and breaking records, but he would never sign an autograph, speak to a fan, give an interview, or speak to the press. He was aloof from his teammates and had this gigantic chip on his shoulder. I hoped that he had mellowed so my son could shake his hand. Forget it. It was if he was all alone, by himself. He would not let anyone near him or talk to him. If people (kids) came over to shake his hand, say hello or ask for an autograph, he would sit stoically, looking straight forward as if the person trying to acknowledge his being was not even there. It was sad to some, disgusting to others. Now, you ask, how about the ladder? How does that apply to Kareem? Well, you see, Mr. Jabbar would undoubtedly have so much to offer a college or professional team. He would be a player's dream, a wonderful coach. He's articulate, experienced and successful. But guess what? He can't get a job. Nobody will hire the man, nobody at all. He simply burned too many bridges. The players have no use for him, the owners won't tolerate him and will never forget, and the press will never forget either. The only ones that are forgiving are the fans, and unfortunately, in this case, it doesn't matter. Fans are always forgiving to the stars, but fans don't hire. Had Kareem been a gentleman, or at least cordial and willing, I believe he would be coaching in the NBA today. Instead, my son and I saw this lonely, sad-looking soul walking in the middle of the street all by himself, away from the crowds of people, exiting the arena. He did everything he could to avoid people, and, by that time, nobody really cared. What a sad sight.

Closer to the real world (the NBA is definitely not the real world), one time, I went to buy a stereo at a big specialty retailer (Best Buy) and I came upon a salesman who treated me like I was a leper. He could care less, had no time, was rude, and so forth. I asked a question and he rolled his eyes like I was a dummy. The phone rang and he answered a personal call and conducted a conversation while I stood there waiting to actually buy something. You know, all the stuff I hate. There's no shock, I'm sure, that I bought somewhere else, but low and behold, a few months later, this piece of garbage comes to see me about a job. Of course, he doesn't recognize me. How could he? He never looked at me when I met him at the stereo store. But I remembered him, and I told him what I thought. I reminded him of our first meeting and told him that he had absolutely no chance of working for me or anyone I knew. I sent him away, tail between his legs, knowing that he had just broken a rung on the ladder of life. Hopefully he learned something, but somehow I doubt it. After all, Kareem didn't. Maybe they never do.

So whats the point? By now, it should be quite clear. You will have your ups and you will have your downs. Somehow, people of the past seem to have a way of popping up in as salesman's future. They tend to be constant or here for awhile and then disappear. Then, they are here again. Buyers are the best example. They seem to just cycle in a salesman's life. They go away and, then, appear somewhere down the road. They kind of make a circuit; a circuit of their own. So, a word to the wise, make sure the last impression was a good one, because no matter what you think today or where you are right now, you may need that person in the future. Cocky arrogance, the kind that sometimes comes with success, tends to haunt us in the future. To you, there will be nothing worse, nothing, than a reunion with a buyer somewhere down the line (or ladder) who thought you were an idiot. Resentment seems to last forever.

MAKE SURE THE LADDER IS STEADY CAUSE YOU MAY HAVE TO USE IT SOMEDAY.

BACK AGAIN ...

In the very beginning of this, I questioned how far this idea of mine would go. "After all," I said, "this is not peddling, and maybe," I continued, "if something comes up that needs to be sold, I may need to take a break and go sell it." Remember, this was at the so-called crossroads that I was so concerned about … facing my 50th birthday while my career seemed to be taking an unexpected turn.

Well, guess what? The birthday has come and gone, as has the great party, complete with the humiliation of Eastern Onion, intent on making a complete fool of me. Actually, people flew in from all over the country to share that great moment of seeing me with a party hat strapped to my head and a half-naked young lady referring to me as someone "over the hill." While this was going on, the inevitable happened as I suspected all along. We found something to sell, and because of it, I haven't paid any attention to this project for more than two months. I guess peddlers are predictable creatures who will agreeably change any path if they have something to sell.

Remembering that I really enjoyed trying to put my thoughts down, I've decided to come back again and pursue this little adventure. As I mentioned, we found something to sell. In fact, our agency, largely due to contacts made through the years and a solid reputation (thank God), is able to attract major opportunities. In this case, as we discussed the professional problems being faced, a major manufacturer contacted us about representing them with their new line of computers. It will be, I strongly feel, a wonderful opportunity.

I mention all this because, once again, I predicted it, and it only proves the expression, to quote my dear old mom, "YOU CAN'T TEACH OLD DOGS NEW TRICKS." Once a salesman, always a salesman. It also further points to a positive attitude as the number one attribute of a successful salesperson. Never stop and never give up! If you handle your career properly and do not let the "DEADLY DISEASE" get you, good things will happen. In this case, the relationships that we made, nurtured, and <u>protected</u> all these years were the basis for this opportunity. The message must be clear to every one of you: Treat people well, regardless of your success. Remember, "WHAT GOES AROUND, COMES AROUND."

I need to tell a great story that should point something out. Later, we are going to discuss the concept of establishing the customers' needs. We all tend to oversell and, in many cases, lose sales because of it. Identifying the "close" is so important, but again, we will discuss that in depth later on. Anyway, this will give you an idea. Because of the new computer line, we felt it appropriate to visit the major retailers and see what they were doing (spying, if you will). It was amazing to see how many customers actually got scared away because the salesperson gave too much unsolicited technological advice. Never once did I hear someone ask appropriate questions regarding the actual intended use of the computer. After all, what was the person trying to do? Why did the customer want a computer?

Here was this nice woman, obviously interested in getting a computer because she had heard so much about them. She was, as most customers seemed to be, a bit scared about the whole thing. I need to add that this was written early in 1994 and all the talk was about the so-called "Information Highway."

At that time, people were a bit nervous, but now, the computer is as commonplace as the telephone.

Anyway, try to take that date into consideration and remember that folks were actually afraid of computers then. Now, back to this woman. She walks into this store and says she wants a computer. Not asking why she wanted one, the salesman begins by showing her a computer and describing the technology. He gets into megabytes, RAM speed, and so on. Visibly confused, she leaves and is probably lost forever. He scared the hell out of her.

In reality, she needed a computer that would write letters and do her checkbook. All the salesman needed to do was ask the question. Another customer was interested in a stereo. Again, the salesman quoted all the technological advantages of his brand and explained the internal devices that made it all work. The customer listened with respect, and after all was said and done, commented that he really wanted one with green lights, not blue. He could have cared less about the internal working parts. He wanted something that looked good. Ask the question and find the need! That is Sales 101.

Enough about me and what I'm doing. We will now continue our journey toward your future. Somehow, someway, someday, I'm liable to get this done.

THE OTHER GUYS

No matter how long we decide to be in this business, there will be two things that no matter how hard we try, we will never change. Everyone we sell to will have our competition selling to them, and everything we sell will have similar items from someone else. Like all of you, I have heard the word or term "exclusive," but honestly, I have yet to really see one in the conventional, normal business channels. If there is a so-called "exclusive," it is generally short-lived at best! So, my friends, you'd better face it. There will always be someone else to compete against. The competitor, fondly referred to by me as THE OTHER GUY, will always be there. Although it is seemingly always a source of concern, in reality, since there is little we can do about it, we shouldn't be bothered. In fact, as I will point out later, it's really good for us. The other guy can, and often does, serve a distinct and important purpose.

How can we as salespeople use the competitor to our advantage? Surely, there is always the fear that what we are trying to peddle may in actuality be similar to some other peddler's wares, and ultimately we may lose the sale (and the commission) to THE OTHER GUY. That is the proverbial risk we all sign on for when we get into this business, and our goal is to always make sure we get our fair share and that other company doesn't. I'll get to the part (eventually) about using the competitor to our advantage. Some salespeople, in fact most of them that I have met and worked with during the years, look at the competitor totally wrong. I guess the word I am looking for is contempt.

But why? In reality, if we are sharp and aware, that other guy could become an ally to us; he could be a giant asset just waiting to help us get the deal done. Remember, the competitor is not an enemy. In fact, he is anything but the enemy. In fact, if treated properly, he or she can become your assistant, in a crazy sort of way. The OTHER GUY is your invaluable source of knowledge. He or she is the manner by which you can construct and plan your sales approach. If handled properly, the competition is all you will ever need to determine "right" and "wrong."

Think about it. All you need to do is read the paper every day, listen to the radio, watch the tube, and guess what? You will see, all day long, what THE OTHER GUYS are doing. They give you all the clues. If you're selling TVs, for example, the newspaper will be full of competitive prices day in and day out. I could go on and on, but I'm sure you get the picture.

How about the direct competitor, the other Rep selling a similar product? He's the guy I see that is normally treated with disdain. That is totally wrong. He too is an ally and a great source of knowledge. Don't ignore this guy or gal. Instead, talk to them; find out what they are doing. Again, the enemy becomes your friend, and you, because you have chosen the road of cordiality, will find another invaluable tool for success. Sit in the lobby and strike up a conversation while you're waiting. Remember, you have two ears and one mouth. You'll want to receive competitive information. You don't want to give out too much. Always keep in mind that it's a fine line and you are a competitor (and source of knowledge) also. I have found that most salespeople (not my guys, not you folks) talk too damn much. They can be a fountain of knowledge. Get it?????

Undisciplined salespeople usually, if not always, have a specific flaw … they love to brag about what they are doing (or are about to do). So many times, in a buyer's lobby, I would hear one of the boys talk about his deals without realizing that perhaps a competitor was over in the corner, supposedly reading *Sports Illustrated*. All the while, however, it wasn't the magazine that was of interest, but rather the dialogue across the room. I would not even try to guess the amount of dollars that turned over, the deals that weren't (and were) made, and the presentations that were changed because some schmuck had a big mouth. What an advantage! In fact, I can recall several times that I was the guy in the corner of the buyers waiting room, reading Sports Illustrated and listening to an actual competitor tip me off as to what he was going to present. I remember on one occasion, a very big deal (in the millions), I listened to this idiot across the room who had this "the deal is mine" attitude, tell another Rep his entire program while I listened, pretending to be reading SI. While he went in and presented his program, I called my factory and completely revised mine. When it was my turn to make a presentation, the program was in the bag. It was the biggest no brainer in history. The other Rep, remember the one with the "this deal is mine" attitude could never figure out how I got the edge on him. It cost him a major program and he was too stupid to realize why he lost it.

Recently, I went to Japan for a visit (non-business). Now, as you may or may not know, the Japanese are very closed-mouthed and extremely coy. They are great at playing business poker. You will never gain an advantage from a Japanese businessman because he runs loose at the mouth. It just does not happen. We Americans, on the other hand, haven't learned yet. Anyway, here I am, having breakfast in the hotel restaurant. Within hearing distance are two American businessmen having breakfast as well. They are busy discussing last night's <u>successful</u> meeting with their Japanese contacts. For all intents and purposes, they are letting everything out on the table within earshot of everyone. How stupid, I thought. If by any chance (and remember, the Japanese are very coy and undoubtedly know about these loose-lipped episode opportunities) a member of last night's group was in the room, the entire deal would be exposed and probably lost. Or if a competitor was nearby, it wouldn't take a whole lot to restructure any presentation to counteract what was being exploited.

Boy, I thought, I wish I were about to make my pitch. I wish I were in this deal. It was laid out for me. An absolute no–brainer, and why? Because these schmucks didn't know how to keep their mouths shut. Here they were, laughing about their exploits, when in reality, the real laugh was on them.

The other guy can be the most valuable asset we have.

THE RISK OF SELLING

There are certainly many positives that are associated with sales. At the same time, there is the inherent risk of working your tail off and winding up with nothing. So many times, days, weeks, and even months are spent in preparation for a sale, only to come away empty-handed. There is simply no guarantee of success. You need to take the risk. It's as simple as that. Although I would like to try to develop a more certain way to make all the work successful, I cannot. There is nothing anyone can do. You simply cannot be successful in sales without adequate discipline and professional preparation and that takes time. I find it very interesting to hear so-called salespeople complain when a sale doesn't materialize after "all the work." Usually, this work is minimal at best. Even if a substantial amount of time is spent, so what? It is part of the game. Frankly, we have no right to complain because the hits are going to outweigh the misses by a very big margin. To be in this game, you need to run the risk of spending a certain amount of time for naught. The realtor drives the people, including the kids, complete with ice cream and sticky fingers, around for days, only to have the customer buy elsewhere or decide not to buy at all. The car salesman goes for the test drive, and perhaps as far as a credit application, only to have the buyer back out or not come back at all. The clothes salesman, the jeweler, the business machine guy ... the list goes on and on. They all take the risk and they all experience the pain of losing "THE DEAL."

Earlier in this chapter, I referred to the salesperson as "so-called." That may sound a bit cold and perhaps that is the perception. I don't mean to be that insensitive. If you work hard on a deal and lose it, I would be the first to sympathize. However, if you are to succeed in this game, you are going to have to get over it quickly. If you cannot take the disappointment, you will never make it in this racket. You will learn to accept this as a fact of life or you will wind up in medical school or some other profession (A doctor, huh? Not bad.).

The "so-called" guy or gal that I am talking about is one that really never does succeed. He or she is so busy complaining and feeling sorry for themselves that they never seem to be able to turn it all around, get that positive attitude back in gear, and go forward. The real "pro" may hitch a bit, but in all actuality, he takes the loss on the chin and rarely complains. Never does he say, "After all this work." HE DOESN'T HAVE THE TIME. He needs to get his act back together more productively and make something work. Quite frankly, the "so-called" person is one that never really puts all that much preparation into something anyway. He or she is too busy complaining.

So, here's the deal. We are going to lose a few, no doubt about it. You are going to bust your tails, do every single thing right, and still lose a deal here and there. You are also going to learn from every experience, keep a positive attitude, and go on with total confidence to the next deal. You are going to win a hell of a lot more than you lose.

THE ROAD

In many cases, those of you who choose sales as a career will, at some time or another, travel as a part of your job. In fact, it should be a foregone conclusion that the road will be home to you at least some of the time. Some will travel a minimal amount, while others, unfortunately, will be gone a great deal.

To many of you, especially those who are just starting out, this may seem glamorous. After all, the thought of flying around the country, arriving at major airports, visiting various "special" club rooms, staying at fine hotels, eating great food at the best restaurants, and so on would seem wonderful. Well, it's not. Sure, traveling and enjoying all the above is terrific for a while, but before long, it becomes very old. Believe me, I've been there and have known hundreds of others who have done the same.

Traveling alone (and that's what you'll do) is a drag, plain and simple. It is a tedious, strenuous, and stressful part of the job. It is not in any way what you imagine it to be. Dinners alone are no fun, my friends! I say that because, to me, that was the worst part of it all. So many nights, I remember sitting by myself, trying to read a book or the paper in an attempt to eat at a decent restaurant (usually in the hotel) and have a good meal. Inevitably, one of two situations seem to always pop up, usually at a table very close by. It is both a man and woman, dining together, enjoying each other's company, or worse yet, a family having dinner together.

Here I am, by myself, alone, and picturing the scene with me in it. I could never help but wonder if they were wondering what the hell I was doing alone anyway. So, now, I'm self conscious. Before long, the entire picture changes and your attempt for a good dinner in a nice restaurant changes to room service or something that you pick up on the way to your room. There are only so many Big Macs or Pizza Hut pizzas one can eat before indigestion becomes an integral part of the road.

You may be asking why, with so many other salespeople, associates, colleagues, and so forth, does one choose to eat alone? That's a good question. The answer, quite bluntly, is that eating with others, after a while, is a pain in the neck. Let's face it, after being on a crowded airplane, rushing through one or two congested airports, dealing with delays, taxis, lost luggage, and several appointments, who the hell wants to eat dinner with people you don't really know? Sure, at first, early in the career, it is tolerable. In fact, you almost are mistaken into thinking you enjoy it. That is until the first time you are thrust into the uncomfortable position of being with a couple (usually your employee or colleague and his wife) that do not get along. The nit picking, under handed insults and sarcastic remarks take a real toll on a dinner. And, after a few drinks, it can become a real mess. I could write an entire chapter on dinners with unhappy couples. After I realized that I was not a shrink, priest or rabii, I decided that I was far better off alone. Before long, you will find every excuse under the sun (I've used them all) to escape the evening's activities. The best excuse, of course, is illness, and I'm always amazed how everyone seems to be so much better the morning after being so sick the night before. It's a miracle! Eating, although a frustration as mentioned above, is nothing compared to some of the other adventures we all discover on the road.

Nothing, absolutely nothing, can test the nerves like flying in airplanes and hanging out at airports. Other than the obvious (near crashes, etc.), air travel is a nightmare. I have always contended that those who run the airlines must stay up at night trying to figure out a way to frustrate and infuriate every business traveler alive. They do nothing, absolutely nothing, to make flying an easy task. Instead, they make it a miserable experience. I could tell you stories that would fill another book. That's not exclusive because it seems for every tale I tell, some other poor "road sucker" can top it.

Years ago, in the early sixties, the airlines catered to the business traveler. There were waived restrictions, tickets that you could write yourself, special clubs, and great fares. It was wonderful, and frankly, travel was pretty easy. Then, for some reason, it all changed and they took away all the benefits that we learned to enjoy. It was as if we were being punished for something. Instead of dealing with a representative of the airline to work with business travelers (and make life easy), we had to work with Travel Agents. Nothing against Travel Agents, but it has become the biggest challenge, and a lifelong one at that, to find one that can consistently perform. Ask a salesperson and you will find total agreement with that statement. It has taken me years to find someone in the travel business that I can count on completely. When she is on vacation, every trip that is handled by her assistant is screwed up. EVERY ONE!

And don't tell me about the Internet. I know it's here and I know it works, but believe me, sales is tough enough without having to search for travel deals; travel deals that change daily. The airport is a world in and of itself. Big city airports are the only places on earth that are more crowded than the streets of India.

Nobody seems to know on what side of the aisle to walk on. Left is right and right is left. The middle is no man's land. And then, without notice, comes the motorized vehicle, carrying people at speeds that rival the Long Island Expressway. I personally have never seen anyone get hurt or hit, but I would bet almost anything that the casualty count is very high.

Luggage is another story altogether. I can't help but argue that we can send people to the moon but we can't seem to figure out a reasonable system for handling luggage! First, everything looks the same nowadays. It used to be that luggage was easily identifiable, but not anymore. Today, when the bags come along the ramp, everyone seems to think it is theirs. Here comes the gray Samsonite and the scramble is on. That is, if the bag gets there at all. Finally, every airport has put into effect what they call "STATE OF THE ART" baggage handling equipment. One is better than the other, they say. Since the emergence of all this new stuff, I swear that it takes at least three times longer than ever for the bags to arrive. "STATE OF THE ART" huh?

I have slept in airports, landed in strange ones, been forced down because of mechanical failure or some other reason, and the most unforgettable one, been involved in a high jacking. (I almost went to Cuba—OLE.) Somewhere around the mid-1960s, high jacking was happening all the time. Highjackers were jumping out of planes in parachutes, etc. They thought it was their way of holding us hostage while presumably trying to go home. Seemed like it was happening every day for a while. At the time, I was traveling a great deal, usually back and forth between New York and L.A. The 747 was new and we loved flying on it. In those days, we (the passengers) were number one and comfort was the priority. We had lounges with baby grand pianos, bars that we could hang out in, and food that was unbelievable. This particular flight was a "Lawry's" special, which meant the famous L.A. restaurant was catering first class with a prime rib cart. They actually walked up and down the first class aisle with a cart of prime rib and cut off the piece you wanted at your seat. Everything was fresh. Everything was first class. Man, it was great, and we, as frequent travelers, only had to pay a small increase to sit up there.

Anyway, here we were, just taking off from Kennedy Airport when the flight attendant, serving us our first glass of champagne, gets seized by this guy who was sitting two rows in front of me on the aisle. At first, it looked like someone was fooling around, but believe me, it was all too serious. The guy who was obviously foreign was holding a knife to a flight attendant's neck. The first class area on the 747 had stairs that went up to the flight deck and he took her up there. The other attendants kept us all cool, but trust me, we needed more than champagne. It only took a few minutes and the captain came on the intercom and announced, "We are under the command of a highjacker. Our course has been changed to Cuba and we have assurances that we will be safe, both from the highjacker and the Cuban government. We hopefully will land in Cuba and return without any problems. Please stay calm, we are under control." No problem! Everyone knew what a great relationship we had with Fidel Castro. Why worry? Bring on the prime rib. It's time to party. I remember, even this many years after, the thoughts that went through my mind. Cuba was not a friend to the U.S. and who knew what would happen once we landed there?

I had a family, a home, a life, and now I was going to Cuba where Fidel Castro preaches hatred of Americans. What a great way to end my week. Yet, somehow, I remained calm and tried to think of it all as an experience. We never got to Cuba. In fact, we never got very far. As I remember the commotion, tumult, excitement, all at lightning-fast speed, our trip was spared by a U.S. Marine who was returning home and refused to go to Cuba. With one quick move, it was over on the bottom step of the staircase in first class. A Marine was standing guard, screaming about not going anywhere but home, and a highjacker, presumably unconscious or worse, was at his feet. The Marine was arrested, the highjacker taken out on a stretcher; half the passengers canceled and went another way (or home), and the rest of us were detained for a few hours and questioned over and again. We were again on our way a few hours later. Here we were, on a plane that was half full, with lots to talk about, and prime rib. Can't remember if I ate any, but the champagne was great.

In spite of it all, the airlines have made no effort to compensate me for these traumas, and despite it all, I still fly. So, it is a necessary evil and one that you, in sales, will learn to live with.

I am not trying to scare anyone away. On the contrary, I am attempting to put the matter of travel in a proper perspective. Too many of us try too very hard to make this part of the job fun. It won't be. It's a drag! So here's the point: Set the entire topic of travel in its proper place and you will do just fine. The entire subject must be treated with respect. You will have no control over some of it (like air travel). The rest is up to you. You may make business trips, you may travel to company meetings, which can be a lot of fun, or perhaps you will begin going to trade shows, which are a lot of work. In any case, you need to come to the mindset that each event is work, not play.

These trips need to be respected, not abused. I have seen careers ended, bright ones at that, because the guy played too hard on the road or partied too much at shows or meetings. Believe me, you will see lots of opportunity for late-night good times, but remember the reasons and objectives of each trip (you are setting them, aren't you?) and the responsibility that you do have. The sooner you do, the better you will do. I am not a prude, believe me. I have seen it all and experienced all the trials and tribulations of the road. The road is a very tough place and you need to be ready, every day. You owe it to yourself and to your employer. As soon as you get that mindset firmly implanted, the road will be tolerable and you will make it just fine. For the most part, every successful guy or gal that I have ever known (big statement) in this business treats the road properly and with respect. They seem to see lots of movies and go to bed early. They are ready, every day, and believe me, they have the edge. HAPPY TRAVELING!

THE *"MAGIC"* OF IDENTIFYING THE NEED

Earlier I mentioned the concept of need as it applies to a customer and how we identify it. This is another example of how everything comes together in sales. Remember how we spoke about listening, having two ears and one mouth? If we listen long enough, we will find the *"MAGIC"* that makes any sale happen. If we know what the customer needs, we should be able to provide a product or service to fulfill that need. In other words, find a need and fill it. If the buyer is looking for red, we would be foolish to offer blue, especially if we knew the need was for red.

This especially applies to problematic situations, and believe me, there will be many. It is part of the game and we as professionals cannot ignore them. To be successful, we need to be able to face problems, assimilate them, and solve them. That is perhaps the most important need your customer will ever have.

I remember so many situations when someone was brought in to put out the proverbial fire, as they say in corporate lingo. A fire is a problem that can be identified easily if the time is taken to identify it. These corporate firemen rarely listened, but went into the meeting full of confidence that they would conquer any problem. It never took long to discover that our hero was in over his head and unprepared for the situation. In almost every case, the meeting was unsuccessful and a frustrating waste of time that left the customer wondering how his or her time could be better spent.

On rare occasion, the pro (that's gonna be you) comes in and takes the time to research and listen. In doing so, he or she finds out the customer's issues, problems, and needs. When he goes into the meeting, he already knows what the customer's problem is, what he is going to accomplish, and if he's smart, has taken the time and precautions to formalize ideas to turn a negative into a positive.

A customer with a problem is interested in absolutely nothing else and certainly nothing new until his problem is resolved. That's always a fact! An example, you ask? Certainly! Many years ago, when I was much younger and a rookie, I worked in the office supply industry, I had an account that was terribly overstocked with a certain item and it was causing the buyer considerable grief. He either over-bought or we over-sold. Whatever the case, he was being hounded daily to get the goods returned. It's not going to take you long in the world of sales to know (if you don't already know) that companies hate to take goods back. Ideally, product sales is a one-way affair. Sell it in and sell it through. Nothing causes the manufacturer more grief than having merchandise returned. It usually has to be handled, reboxed, repacked, and so forth. Companies hate it, plain and simple. In this case, the customer was a big one (they all are) and I was given the directive to "solve the problem or else!" I never knew what "or else" meant, although I sure heard it often in the early days when the customer thought I could be intimidated (which I was, quite easily).

I took the local "senior" guy to the account to try to get this thing resolved. He made no attempt to find out the details. In fact, he didn't want to know. His philosophy was to "shoot from the hip," as he called it, and solve problems on the spot. You guessed the result. There was no result. In fact, the customer was no longer upset, but irate. I was told to get the deal done or (again) "or else."

So, I called my Sales Manager, a fellow that I totally respected and admired. He hired me, trained me, and in many ways, made me what I am today. I needed help and, as a young guy, I had no experience. He was a pro in every sense of the word. I'll mention his name, Bill Atherton, in the hope that maybe someday he will come upon this writing. When he arrived, he suggested that before going on the call, we sat down for a little while. He wanted to review the situation. He went over every single detail of the sale and what had transpired since. He wanted everything, especially the temperature (another sales term) of the buyer.

We went on the call, meeting a very upset customer who had been stalled far too long. His manager was on his case and his job was on the line. My boss got right to the point, spending almost no time on small talk. That was, as I look back, his style under any circumstance, good or bad. He already knew the problem and everything that had occurred up to that minute. Yet, acting as if he knew nothing, he asked the buyer to relate the issue at hand. We listened for much longer than I would have anticipated. By doing so, I discovered new issues and concerns I had never before heard. That was probably because I hadn't taken the time before now.

The buyer said the bottom line was that he had bought the goods in good faith, but they hadn't sold. He wanted them out before he could continue doing business with our firm. He felt it was our responsibility, which I learned to realize, is always the case with dead goods. I'd like to find one single buyer that ever took the blame for slow sales. That's what we're here for! Part of what we heard this time was an issue that was really bothering the buyer, one that I hadn't heard or realized before … the subject of lost profit and the fact that he was accountable.

Bill let him finish and then suggested that he had a resolution. He explained that he felt the buyer wanted out of the problem but did not necessarily want to return the goods. After all, if he could sell the goods at a profit, he would be a hero in the eyes of his management. If he simply sent them back, he would be looked upon as a buyer who made a bad mistake.

"You wouldn't want that perception, would you?" Bill said in the most matter-of-fact way, and he continued, "We wouldn't want that to happen to you." He went on to assure the buyer that he could make him a hero and solve his problem. Instead of returning the goods, a plan was made to promote the goods with extra promotional dollars and a decrease in price that we would share equally. The thought here was that the customer would be happy with some profit instead of no profit. He agreed! The promotional dollars would be generated as a tradeoff for the money the company would have had to spend to take the goods back. Without getting into the details of the promotion, Bill figured out a way to eliminate the problem profitably and, at the same time, sell the customer more merchandise. Yes, you heard me, we walked out of there with another order, a big smile on our faces, a very happy customer, and (for me) a lifelong lesson learned.

The company we worked for would not be forced to take the goods back and we would not be faced with having to try. Instead, we all won … the customer, the factory, and us. Hooray for the good guys! All this was accomplished <u>only</u> because the time was taken to listen and analyze the customer's needs.

This situation, which happened quite early in my career, has left a lasting impression on me. I have used it as a template for situations that have occurred throughout my career. It was a lesson that I learned and one that I have passed on to dozens of people that I have had the pleasure to manage. You need to learn that a vital factor, perhaps the most vital factor, in selling something is to find a need and fill it. The only way to find that need is to listen. Where have we heard that before!

WHO CARES?

Regardless of our chosen profession, we are all human beings and human beings have problems. We all suffer the same conflicts and have similar frustrations. Salespeople, however, being the types that we are, tend to let our emotions show more than others. Being out in the public negates the chance that others have of hiding their problems behind their desks. We need to always be aware of this because it can (and often does) affect our business.

Your problems are, naturally, important to you at the time that they are occurring. None of us can predict when and where a personal problem occurs. Arguments with the spouse, a traffic ticket on the way to work, the unsympathetic boss, a bad cold, a headache, the flu, and so on. All these things and the hundreds of other situations that happen to us can disrupt the productivity of your day (days) if you are not careful.

It takes a great deal of discipline (where have we heard that before?) and constant attention to our moods to make certain these situations do not cause adverse affects. The point I am vividly trying to make is a simple one: Your problems are yours alone. Nobody really cares about them. No matter what a customer may say, he could care less. Despite the fact that only a fool would discuss problems with customer (no fools here, I hope), unless a conscious effort is made, your mood, good or bad, is instantly recognized by the customer. If for any reason, your mood is poor, it will and does affect the sales call. The customer is automatically turned off. Trust me, it happens every single time.

Bottom line (oh, that old bottom line) is that regardless of what you may think of your relationship with a business associate, the real truth is that he or she has problems too. They could care less about yours. So, dunk your head in cold water, slap yourself in the face, jump around, go to church ... whatever it takes. Just get yourself out of it before you make the call or don't go. By the way, all of the slapping, jumping, church garbage ... it's all been tried, tested, and proven successful. Me personally? I used the slap! Some days, especially in the beginning, the old face was really sore, but the customer was spared the boredom of my personal mood degenerators.

Now, let's turn the tables. You go to see the customer and he/she is in a shitty mood (sorry, there simply is no other word suitable for a bad mood buyer). You recognize it instantly, detect the attitude, and realize that this is not your day. But you are there! If you have traveled thousands of miles and you have no choice, you need to bite the bullet and hope for the best. Don't push too hard and don't try to tell the buyer he is wrong about anything. And, by the way, it may not be a good idea to initiate conversation about the spouse. Chances are, the spouse is the problem that is making your butt twinge. Just soft peddle the deal, be as light tempered as you can, and hope for the best. If you have not traveled thousands of miles and rescheduling does not create too much of a problem, simply find an excuse and split.

The excuse can be something very believable. For example, you have suddenly developed a major stomachache and the runs are imminent.

Bottom line ... nothing is worse than a buyer in a bad mood, not even the runs!

THE BANK PRESIDENT AND "THE SHARK"

Somewhere around the beginning of this book, I wrote a chapter called

"THE PRETENDERS AND THE ENEMY." It must be one of my favorite topics, or at least one that I am most adamant about because I keep coming back to the subject. Remember, I'm the guy working to gain professional respect for the salesperson. Aren't we getting tired of the old lowlife treatment?

A few years ago, while standing in line at a movie theater here in beautiful Scottsdale, Arizona, I met one of my heroes. Most of you know who Harvey Mackay is. For those who may not, he is a syndicated author who writes sales "stuff" in every major paper every Sunday. He has written several books that are bestsellers in their genre. One of the books, *Swim with the Sharks Without Being Eaten Alive,"* has gained Mackay worldwide notoriety. I suppose this is the reason why he now has the national column. The book led to a software program called *"Sharkware."*

I fondly refer to Harvey as "The Shark" and he loves it. We have corresponded a few times and he always closes the letters he sends me with, "Keep Swimming." On top of all that, Harvey owns Mackay Envelope Company, which was, as he willingly tells anyone, his beginning to all this greatness. This is not in any way sarcastic because Harvey Mackay is one of my most admired professionals. As I mentioned, I met Harvey in a movie line. Recently, he wrote an article about his reaction to a situation that involved a bank. Basically, he expressed his opinion that all employees are salespeople and that banks need to recognize that. As you can guess, I took aim at Harvey's view, expressing my firm opinion that all employees were not, in any way, salespeople, and that if we were to gain the respect due us, we better start realizing that.

You know the pitch. I go on and on about it. Frankly, I was surprised to hear that from a guy like Harvey Mackay who gets paid big money to speak on motivational subjects. Does he really think that all employees are salespeople? I wrote to Harvey and expressed my concerns. I mentioned the guys at McDonald's selling Big Macs and the gal at 7-Eleven.

He responded with a thank-you letter and no real answer to my concerns, leading me to believe that Harvey Mackay, the old Shark himself, thinks the clerk at 7-Eleven is a salesperson. What a shockeroo! I was certain that I could find an ally in Harvey. Surely, he shared the same professional pride that I do. What a surprise! Then again, maybe I embarrassed him and he just could not bring himself to admit thinking the girl at the drive-up window at Bank of America was a salesperson. Deep down, I thought (and still do) that Harvey Mackay knows what I am saying and agrees with me. I trust we will have the chance to debate the issue a bit more, maybe at the next movie. I must also consider the aspect of dollars as it relates to audience. I suppose, the more people you include in the category of "sales," the more people will buy your books. I know that my minimizing the clerk-type as I have done here so adamantly does reduce my prospective clientele. In fact, some of my critics have expressed that very thought, but what can I say? I am what I am, and I believe what I believe. I can't be all things to all people. The money is just not that important.

So, this leads me to yesterday when I went to lunch with my banker. While chomping on the Caesar salad, he mentioned that the president of his bank sent out a message to all personnel earlier that day expressing the old "Harvey Mackay" opinion that all of them, every one, were *sales*people. Apparently, his feeling was that in order to improve their stature in the marketplace, they had to take a sales approach to their clients. "It was easy," he said, "we are all salespeople and we must conduct ourselves as such."

"What the hell does that mean?" I commented rather quickly and curtly. Well, as you can guess, that was the end of my Caesar salad and my lunch. At the risk of choking with a mouth full of Caesar salad, there was no way that I was going to let this conversation end without a few choice comments because I knew that this philosophy was totally unrealistic and anything but sincere or thought out. That's the problem with someone like Harvey sending out the wrong message.

I asked a simple question, preempted by urging my lunch date to be as honest as he could be. I could not be offended, I assured him. My question asked how he perceived the average salesperson. After minimal urging, he admitted that he saw us as the high roller, stereotypical, WKRP in Cincinnati, yellow jacket, green pants radio guy! Further urging brought about all the negative things that people see in salespeople, all the things that make us look like we are not professionals. He went on to talk about the "Used Car Syndrome" and all the other goodies we all hear so often. In fact, once he started, he couldn't stop. Exploiting the sales "type" had become fun! Man, did I wish Harvey was with us now. What a lesson he'd soon learn. Fodder for a new, revised column.

I asked him if he thought this stereotype was typical of people in the financial community, perhaps his boss? He emphatically agreed that it was. Why then, I asked, would his boss, the bank president, want his financial-type employees to be salespeople when, clearly, there was little or no respect for them (except for the dinero they deposit)? Why, I asked, would they want to emulate the guy from WKRP or, my favorite, the Tin Man? You should have seen the look on his face. He was puzzled that these questions were so intriguing.

Here's the real point: How many current employees really want to be salespeople? If they did, they wouldn't be current employees, would they? Oh sure, they all think they could be in sales. Can't everyone? But they would be different. They would be the conservative salesperson. You know my answer to that one. Why not hire salespeople instead of the MBAs on staff? Why is there not one "Sales Type" in the entire organization? Aren't we talking about a real paradox? On one hand, Mr. President wants his people to become salespeople, but on the other, he would never hire a salesperson. The only sales guy or gal that would be acceptable by a bank would be one that has an MBA and, frankly, I don't see too many sales-oriented types getting one. So, I ask, what's the deal?

Certainly, there are some salespeople in every bank, but all bank employees are not (and should not be) considered salespeople. Mr. President, it is not that simple. Working with the public takes not only courage, but also talent. Throwing a non-sales type into sales is asking for trouble. If you need salespeople, hire a few! Trust me, we don't wear pink jackets and yellow pants. Some of us speak quite well and can work with financial figures. (This might come as a big shock, but a sales gal or guy can add, count money, and give change, all the while smiling and promoting the business.) The financial people that graduated with degrees in Accounting, Finance, etc., do not want to be salespeople or they would have become salespeople. Seems pretty simple to me.

So, while still at lunch, I concluded that the perception was that the bank employees were, in effect, selling the bank and should act accordingly. (I'm on a big roll now.) That is true, but actually, they are representing the bank, not selling. To do this, all they need to do is brush up on their cordiality, professionalism, and personality. Then, I believe Mr. President will have what he is looking for … a bank represented by friendly, caring people. Imagine having people like us working in the bank. Every customer would love to deposit their hard earn dolero's at the world's most friendly, congenial, and professional place. The "I don't know" attitude is replaced by the very simple "sure we can."

These are not salespeople. Sales is a profession. We are, at least those of us who have earned it, professionals with credentials that prove it. We're not bankers and bankers are not salespeople but we all have one thing in common, the common desire to treat customers "right." In that respect, I concluded, perhaps we can all learn something from watching WKRP in Cincinnati. "Oh yeah," said my lunch guests, "that's it, isn't it?" I watched him as he shook his head in disbelief that, in fact, that really was it, quite simply. We don't need an MBA to figure that one out.

MAKING APPOINTMENTS

It's part of the game, like it or not. To become successful in sales, you are going to have to learn to make appointments. It is not as easy as it may seem. In fact, it gets increasingly more difficult as time goes by. Why? First, today's buyer is in no way equal to the buyers of years ago. They are no longer paid the kind of dollars that they used to be paid and now the professional merchant is not attracted to the buying world. Those that are seem to be few and far between, "hangers-on" to the past.

Today's buyer, in many cases, does not know the business, nor does he or she realize the importance of a Rep or salesperson. Therefore, what used to be the appointment (face to face) with a buyer has now become, in many cases, a faxed presentation or a sample sent by the factory to an assistant. Today's world, filled with technology and the toys that go with it, has created this situation. The buyer no longer needs to be as qualified, and we (the salespeople) are forced to present long distance.

A few weeks ago, I called a local retail supermarket asking for an appointment. I was told by an assistant that the buyer did not have time to meet with me and that I should send information on the item to her. She would in turn show the buyer, and if there was any interest, they would call me. In this case, I complied, but under most conditions, I would not have. More about that in a minute when I discuss what I should have done. In this case, however, I really didn't care. It's as simple as that. As you can imagine, no phone call was made to me, and consequently, the item was not bought.

Yesterday, I had lunch with the buyer's boss (Merchandise Manager) and I asked if his company was going to buy that specific item. He told me that they were, in fact, buying it for the Fall quarter of the year. I then pursued it a bit further, finding out that the item they bought was considerably higher than the one I sent and the quality was not as good. We further learned that my presentation was never opened. You might guess that the manager was very upset and <u>will</u> take action to rectify the situation.

Bottom line on the above situation is that the buyer should see everyone. It is her or his professional responsibility, not only to the company he or she works for, but most importantly to their customer. Unfortunately, it does not work that way. Instead, we are asked to send a proposal in writing, one that quite often isn't opened. This brings us back to the original topic, making appointments.

The key to getting an appointment is strength. You need to have conviction and you cannot give in. If a buyer won't give you an appointment, then you should not send in a proposal. If you are talking about a long-distance situation, then that's different, but if we are talking about a local, territorial account, there is no excuse. You should be seen! You will have to learn how to convince the buyer to give you the time. It's just too easy to just send something.

The key is to minimize the time you will need from them. Ask for only five minutes. Tell whoever is on the phone that you have something to show them, it's not something you want to send, and you're only asking for five minutes. Do not, I repeat, do not present the item on the phone. I have always told the buyer that I was the worst phone salesman in the world. It would be unfair to the buyer (and to me) to force a phone presentation. Surely, they have five minutes to spare. I would continue by saying, "If you force me to talk about this on the phone, I will be cheating myself and you." Remember, stay strong, and don't give in. If you don't give up, you will win, and you will get the appointment. Also, a written presentation without personal contact is normally the kiss of death. If you are forced to do so, make sure you personally speak with the buyer (not the assistant) and sell the item big-time before sending anything. My motto: *NO BUYER, NO PRESENTATION.*

TODAY I LOST A HERO

Believe it or not, it's been a couple of years since I wrote even a single word in this project of mine. A great deal has happened to me since then. Since my last thoughts were written, we have moved to Scottsdale, Arizona. I have started a new business and have succeeded in a new venture. More about that later. In fact, I am going to devote an entire chapter to that, but for now, I need to deal with something else.

Today I learned that an old colleague of mine has passed away. His name was Leonard and he is one of the very few people I will mention by name in this book. I would mention his last name, but I fear it would have embarrassed him, so let's just leave it at "Leonard."

I have had few heroes in my life. Leonard was one of the few and an unlikely hero he was. Leonard was rough, tough, somewhat insensitive, and outwardly rude, even to me. He was about five foot nine inches in height and weighed I would guess 400 pounds, believe it or not. He looked like a big stump. His eyes drooped and he looked like a big bulldog. Yet from the very first day, there was magic, special magic, between him and me. I still don't know why. He wasn't particularly nice to me. I was just one of many, at least at first. I met the man when he became president of an aluminum cookware company located in Wisconsin. The company, a big name for sure, had been on the verge of bankruptcy with a reputation that was lower than its bank account. They were hated for lots of reasons. Leonard, with this reputation preceding him, was hired to straighten it out and was being paid a great deal of money to do so. Despite the poor reputation and horrible financial condition, once the "old man" was hired, the confidence level soared. For some reason, all the national talent wanted to jump on board. Leonard, in spite of what he was, apparently held lots of clout. That is not to say that he was well liked. No, more like "well respected from a distance."

As a housewares Rep, I heard that the line was available. I was not very successful at the time. In fact, struggling is probably the proper word to describe exactly where I was. This line would be a big name for me, and despite the lack of volume and presence in the market, I wanted it badly. As you might have guessed by now, when I wanted something badly, I usually got it. After being hired, I was sent to Manitowoc, Wisconsin (known later as Outer Mongolia), for two reasons: (1) to train; (2) to meet, firsthand, the "old man."

Leonard met us at the hotel on the first day. He was polite, although a bit distant. There were about 50 Reps at the meeting, most not knowing what or who to expect. We had dinner and then it happened! Leonard made a speech, and frankly, it was the very moment that I was hooked. I had a hero. He was the absolute very best speaker I had ever heard. He was simply the best. By the time he was done, there wasn't a dry eye in the room. Leonard had arrived ... Leonard owned us all. The rest is history. Within two years, this company became the biggest, best, and most successful housewares company in the world. Did Leonard do it? Not by himself, but believe me, he was the leader and he made it happen.

When something impossible had to be done, he got it done, every time.

There were many Leonard speeches after that first. Everyone was wonderful, overwhelming, and ended with a room full of tears. He talked about motherhood, America, and us. Two years after we all started, we had a meeting in Chicago. Over 500 people were present at McCormick Place. Leonard established an award, THE EAGLE. It was for the Sales Rep of the Year and this speech topped them all. In a darkened room with eagles soaring on the screen, a song about eagles in the background, and "The Old Man" prominently displayed at a podium, talking about the eagle as the most majestic, most powerful, most wonderful symbol there could be. *"To soar with the eagles, you had to be special. Not everyone could, not everyone should."*

In this case, Leonard said there was only one. Unexpectedly, the "only one" was me. It was without any doubt the highlight of my professional career. I will never forget Leonard's presentation and the way I received my Eagle, a Stubben crystal piece, still displayed proudly in my home. I stood at the podium, listening to the group cheering. As I looked at Leonard, he suddenly seemed seven feet tall. He smiled at me, gave me a hug, and said, "Thank you." Afterward, as we walked alone together, I asked why he thanked me. I felt that I should be thanking him and he said, "No, my son. You see, *some people are rained on and some people make it rain. You are a rainmaker."* I will never forget that statement or that day. I will never forget Leonard. He was our friend. He risked everything for principle in spite of the consequences.

He, all alone and all by himself, stood up for us to the world's biggest account, WAL-MART, whose president sent a memo to all manufacturers INSISTING ON THE ELIMINATION OF Reps and, most specifically, their commission. Ninety-nine percent of all manufacturers either changed their structure or began sending owners, NOT REPS, to Wal-Mart, but Leonard said NO! He risked losing millions to the account in order to keep his honor because, as you may have guessed, Leonard was a peddler. Not a PhD, not an MBA, but a peddler. And may this peddler rest in peace and find someone new to sell!

A HOT DOG STAND IT IS!

I'm not sure if I told you this, but I grew up in Chicago, home of the Cubs, Bears, Bulls, deep dish pizza, ribs, and the absolute ultimate hot dog—the CHICAGO DOG. How can a hot dog be famous, you ask. Try this for an answer. There is a very famous place in Chicago called Navy Pier. It used to be an extension of The University of Illinois, and is now converted into a mile-long (or more) pier protruding out from Michigan Avenue. It's full of some of Chicago's best nightspots and an amusement park. In and of itself, it is very famous. One of the best-selling posters in the world is one depicting Chicago's skyline with Navy Pier in the foreground, but the actual pier is replaced by a Chicago Dog with all the trimmings. I grew up on those babies. I can taste them right now, steaming hot on a poppy seed bun (lightly steamed as well), covered with mustard, the greenest, sweetest relish anyone has ever tasted, onions, pickles, tomatoes, peppers, and something called celery salt. Oh boy! My mouth is watering on my keyboard.

You are probably wondering how this sales guy, your peddler buddy, is suddenly into green relish (unbelievable, trust me) and soft steamy buns. What the hell is next? As you know (or will know as you get older), some things, certain people, and special times play a very important role in your lives. These usually happen sometime in your youth and have found a way to penetrate the old brain and stay there forever. It stays quiet deep inside there, but every once in a while it pops up.

Strange that a hot dog would pop up like that, but in my case, it does and always has. You are baffled! This guy is crazy. First, he writes about sales stuff and now green relish

71

(the greenest—has to be a certain kind). You're waiting for the punch line. What the hell is this guy trying to peddle now? You know my MO. There is always a point!

So here's the deal, the real deal: As I became successful, along with the success came all the frustrations that go with all the trappings. Some of the frustrations and problems are easier to solve than others. Some, once conquered, go away forever, but others seem to reappear over and again. The older we get, the worse these things are and so we begin to long for the dreams, innocent dreams, of days long ago. We yearn for what was then, not what is now. Now is frustrating, troublesome, stressful, and gives you gray hair (if the buyers have allowed you to keep a few strands by now), and sleepless nights.

Uh oh … I bet you're beginning to smell that relish yourself. Told you there is a method to my madness. As I grew up in Chicago, these hot dog stands and their distinctive odor were quite prevalent, each one better than the last one. We would eat there often. What a treat! Ultimately, I grew to realize that these generated pretty darn good money, all cash, and all year long.

A simple business making a lot of money. Pretty good concept—don't you think?

Back to these frustrations … the longer I was in business, the more these memories snuck out to remind me of my past. My travels took me to Chicago several times a year. On every occasion, at least one or two visits to these hot dog stands would be absolutely necessary. I must have introduced literally hundreds of people to this Chicago delicacy and each one, WITHOUT FAIL, would see fit to return on future visits and would talk about it, just like I did.

As the frustrations grew greater, I would threaten my associates with my dream … the dream (threat) of leaving all the bullshit and opening a CHICAGO HOT DOG STAND. Sometimes, at least for the first couple of dozen years, I said it in jest, but as time went by, I was more serious. When it became most intolerable, and it did, I would say things like, *"One of these days, I'm gonna walk away from all this and open a hot dog stand."* All the while, I was quite serious.

Well, folks, be careful what you wish for because it just might come true. For the past ten years, I have been selling hot dogs made in Chicago and cooked to perfection in my restaurant in Arizona. It's not the prototypical Chicago Hot Dog Stand. I've never been accused of doing anything the easy way! It's a full-blown, sit-down diner with booths, shakes, bar stools rock 'n' roll music ('50s), and 150 menu items including HOT DOGS! Yep, I walked away from all the bullshit and called their bluff. No more buyers, no more airplanes no more commissions that don't arrive on time. Do I miss it? Not a bit. Why should I? I'm fulfilling my dream, my hot dog fantasy, and I'm making some money, too!

THINGS AREN'T BAD—THINGS HAVE CHANGED

At some point in time, there is going to be a crisis that is going to affect your business. It can create minimal damage or it can have a major effect that could put you out of business.

On September 11, 2001 (known as 9-11), the United States was attacked at its core by terrorists. We all know the story, reiterating it is not for this moment. Suffice it to say, it set this country and the world on its proverbial ear. It will take so many years to assess the real damage. We will be evaluating the changes created as well as the hidden damages for more years than any of us will be around.

I was in the restaurant business, running my diner and growing, when 9-11 hit, and like so many others, I was faced with a personal crisis. After realizing what had been done and coming to grips with it, I had to set a direction for my business, one that would be effective and overcome the negative tone that was encircling every business and the entire nation. The economy was becoming a secondary problem to the fear that we were experiencing. Suddenly, those of us who were independent because of the flourishing economy prior to 9-11 were feeling a twinge of fear (you know that feeling and where it generates from) about the future of our families, our retirement, and our daily bills.

Things were falling apart. We were all the victims and we were hurting.

So, the obvious was going to be facing us in business. We were going to see unemployment rise, spending tighten, and attitudes fade. As a businessman, I had to react. I had to sit back and use everything that I had learned to see how people were going to react.

Theories began forming everywhere and I listened to them all. Remember,I have two ears and only one mouth (previous chapter). Most people in the restaurant business felt that in order to survive, they would have to compromise. They cut staff and the costs related to payroll, cut portions and lowered food costs, and in most cases, eliminated promotional opportunity for the guests. This theory proved to be the death of many restaurants. The real problem is that people who frequent a certain place become used to the way it operates and they expect certain things. When those things disappear, especially in times of crisis, the guest becomes insulted and he or she goes elsewhere. By the time we recoup our poor judgment, it's too late. We have shown our colors. We have committed professional suicide. By the way, this poor judgment is not exclusive to one industry. Most businesses in most fields did the same.

On the other hand, my philosophy was diametrically different. My decision was to "kill 'em with service like never before." It was time to wine and dine, as they say. I decided to make sure that when a guest came into my place, they left totally and completely satisfied. Instead of cutting corners, we broadened them. Instead of decreasing staff, we added people. Anyone not doing their job was cut and they knew it. Instead of cutting portions, we increased them. The result was increased business and growth instead of deterioration.

This only attests to the ongoing philosophy that I have had forever: BUSINESSES ARE BUILT IN THE FRONT OF THE HOUSE. Accountants, engineers, warehouse managers, product managers, and so on do not build businesses. No, my friends, it's us, PLAIN AND SIMPLE.

It boils down to good old customer service, making the consumer feel like they are the most important person in the world. If things are bad, it's only natural to cut, but the customer has no idea that things are bad. What the customer does realize is that things have changed and they resent that. So, we decided to give the best service ever, to give the best quality anywhere. We grew! We survived! Others, many others, did not.

And now, I'll let you in on a little secret. In order to do all those things to improve quality and service, I had to raise prices incrementally. I did it and nobody even noticed. We paid for all the good stuff but the service overcame everything. Service always overcomes everything.

Here's the real point, maybe the point of this entire book. Money and success are not attained by counting pennies. Money takes care of itself if you take care of the customer. Businesses are built by service. It makes no difference what kind of business you're in. It's all the same. If you're selling as a Rep, the buyer expects to be your priority. If you make him or her feel like he or she is, then you will succeed. It's that simple. If you are in the restaurant business, it doesn't make a damn bit of difference what you pay for a head of lettuce. In fact, if you bet me $1,000, I could not tell you the price of a head of lettuce. What difference does it make anyhow? What matters is that every guest feels your presence and they know that you are honored to have them in your place. What matters most is that they are taken care of. It's really that simple. In the long scheme of things, the price of a head of lettuce, or a case, is not what brings the people back. The people come back because of you and the way your standards are set. It may not be a head of lettuce but, its all the same. You, your standards and how you treat your customers is what will make you succeed.

SOME THINGS ARE TAKEN FOR GRANTED

Every time I try to end this thing, something else happens and I feel compelled to write about it. Hopefully, the end is near and you folks can put this down and go about the task at hand … making a fortune by using some of this stuff. Anyway, the other night, I was invited along with my wife and a few friends to The Harmon Killebrew Charity Golf Outing Auction and Dinner. It was at a country club, and we had the pleasure of meeting some of my old baseball heroes. In case I haven't mentioned it before, I am a huge baseball fan, a student of the game, and I follow it like clockwork. In fact, the next book I write is going to be about the game. Since I was a very little boy, since I saw my first real ballpark and its splendid grass playing surface and the smell that only a ballpark can have, I have followed the game and I have accumulated numerous heroes.

Harmon, in case you don't know, is one of the greatest players ever. Famous in the '50s and '60s, Mr. Killebrew hit 573 home runs, is a Hall of Famer, and is so respected that he is the actual silhouette logo on every piece of baseball gear sold in the world. He is a very big deal and a very wonderful guy. I first met him in my restaurant and the relationship has grown from there. Great guy!

So here I am at this dinner and I am in proverbial "Baseball Heaven." It is, without any doubt, a highlight, one of my greatest thrills. I am meeting and talking to legends that I grew up watching on TV. Names like Bob Fellar, Brooks Robinson, and Tony Oliva are sitting with me and I am introducing my wife and son to these legends.

Maybe they don't really understand the significance of the meetings, but I am explaining who, what, where, and how in every case. After a bit, they catch on that they are in the midst of something very great, very special (especially to me) and a once-in-a-lifetime situation. After the initial euphoria of the moment, I sit back and realize something. These guys don't play anymore! These guys are old, some of them ill. The once great hands now have arthritis. These guys, if you had no idea who they were, would appear to be regular guys, most of whom are a little out of shape. What a revelation. Even the great ones get old. Even the superstars get fat and bald. I could not help to finally realize what Paul Simon meant when he wrote and sang, "*Well here's to you Joe DiMaggio, Jesus loves you more than you will know.*" And so it goes. These guys will always be special to me and millions of others who recognize them or are introduced to them, but the truth is, they are really just men. I started to get a bit emotional, realizing what I was experiencing. It simply boiled down to simplicity. They had a job to do and they did it better than the others. They were the best at what they did, and after they accomplished their goals, it was their time to leave and let someone else, people like Barry Bonds, A Rod and Randy Johnson, carry on in their names. So, they succeeded and became famous. They left the others behind, and I thought to myself, I did that too. I did my job, better than most, and left the others behind. Hey, if there were a Sales Hall of Fame, I'd probably be in it. Think of that! And I thought of all of you … my friends who have been my students for ten years now. You also have a chance to leave the others behind, to excel as the best. You have a chance to make the Hall of Fame too.

You're no different, no better or worse than Bob Fellar, who threw the first 100-mile-per-hour fastball. Our art is just a bit different. One day, we'll all look back, a little less fit, a little more bald, and we'll see the new guys coming up the ladder we are climbing now. And you'll smile like I did when I hugged Harmon and said good night.

A FORMULA FOR WINNING

"When all the facts are gathered and all the dice are thrown, it's the guy or gal who *writes the most business that makes the most money and ultimately gets the most respect."*

I have often used athletic teams as a model for businesses in general. Running a company or a sales team is, in so many ways, similar to running a football or baseball team. Many components have to work independently, as well as in conjunction with each other. Think about it as you go and the comparisons will become more and more noticeable.

One of the greatest football coaches of all time is Joe Gibbs. As of the date of this writing, he is the coach of the Washington Redskins. This will be his first year after coming out of retirement. No kidding, Joe Gibbs retired several years ago to spend the rest of his life enjoying the fruits of his success. His team, the Redskins, was more than successful under his tutelage, but since his departure, and in spite of the efforts of several head coaches, all very well known, they have failed. So, the Redskins convinced Joe Gibbs to come back out of retirement. Trust me, he will succeed. He is a winner!

Recently, Joe was asked about his formula for winning. I believe the question was, *"What makes a winner?"* Most people would think that the answer would have something to do with the talent and ability of the players. He did not say that. Instead, he said that winners were made because the players were smart. It was their ability to make the right decisions that made them, and ultimately the team, winners. Being smart on the field is, in his opinion, the answer to success.

How does that relate to sales? If serving donuts or being a clerk at a convenience store is not sales, then how in the world can playing football be sales? It does relate.

During the years that I sold, operated sales teams, managed companies, and so forth, the consistent factor, or at least one of them, was that people got hired because they were capable. Isn't it a "given" that those who make the NFL are talented, far more talented in their field than most? It's the same in sales. If you are hired, it's because you have the talent, at least in the eyes of the management. I know that can be another story altogether because there is the possible element of a weak manager who really should not be hiring. *Some perhaps should be serving donuts*! This is probably another chapter all its own, but I need to note that I have seen some of the most incompetent people in charge of others (usually also incompetent). Suffice it to say, poor, inadequate management almost always leads to either a forced restructuring or bankruptcy. Nothing is worse. Ever heard the expression *"shit rolls down hill"?* (Well, that is the expression) It basically means that everything starts at the top, and if management sucks, everything else usually does as well. I have wondered many times about who the hell hired the managers that ultimately hired the inept salesperson who is working with the customer. If you analyze it, to guys and gals like us, IT'S SO EASY TO WIN. The competition usually stinks. One factor is that ineptitude in the business world, specifically in the field of sales, has not changed one iota since I started. It was bad years ago and is still bad. Same problem, different people.

I remember when I first started in the Rep business and called on a major supermarket chain. I met a buyer, Charlie, who was a great guy, although, I was always sure that he did not want anyone to know it, but I did. He really helped me get started, and I think the bottom line was that he was a street fighter like me; different time and different street, but street fighters the same. We clicked. So one day, he tells me this story, trying to give me his interpretation of why I was going to be VERY successful in his opinion (which he valued highly). He said, *"Lee, you do something really unique in this day and age."* I asked what that was and he said, *"You ask for the order."* Imagine that. He went on to tell me that most so-called salesmen bring in the sample, make a presentation, and then leave. And Charlie then goes to the buying committee to present the item.

A week or so later, the salesman comes back and picks up his samples. Charlie proceeds to ask the person, *"So, don't you want to know if I'm going to buy?"* They would usually reply that they had thought he would have told them. That alone should make them a candidate for the lingerie department at Nordstrom's. I, on the other hand, would call Charlie and tell him when I was coming over to PICK UP THE ORDER. He loved it! All buyers love to be asked for the order, but most so-called salespeople never do ask (orders are not a gift). And you want to know why winning is easy? Some manager has to hire these order takers. Been to a movie theatre lately? The folks behind the counter serving (note that I did not say selling) popcorn and candy had to be hired by someone, presumably a manager. These are the worst customer-oriented people in the world. They are just plain rude and usually so animated that it's gross. Almost every time I go to a movie, I want to report them to someone, but to whom would I report them? I can just picture the ad that they must be running in the papers.

> *"If you are rude, insensitive, obnoxious, and incapable of talking in a realistic tone, then we have a perfect job for you. Call ABC Theatres. No interview required. See the manager on duty."*

It's similar to the ad that is run for the Department of Motor Vehicles, any one of them, anywhere. Who ever worked at a Department of Motor Vehicles with a personality that included a smile? As for me, every time I visited a DMV to pay my fees (usually ridiculous), I walked away feeling like someone who had just done something very bad. After standing in a seemingly endless line, you are moved along when numbers are called by this geek behind the counter who has no qualms about telling you that you have been standing in the wrong line all along or have forgotten something necessary to complete the process. Oh yeah, there's no way can you run to the car and get the forgotten piece of paper or documents and go to the front of the line. Sorry, it wouldn't be fair to the next guy. You gotta be kidding me!

Then, there is always the chance that one of the employees (or two) takes a break right in the middle of everything, when the line is at its maximum length. They feel no shame in simply closing their window and walking off, without so much as an expression, a look upward, or a word. It's just a sign on the window after the clock strikes the exact moment that a break is due. I have actually seen people go ballistic at this point. Then there are the people who work at insurance companies. FORGET ABOUT IT! Talk about an exercise in futility! Most of them can't even speak! It feels like you're talking to someone from a foreign country. In fact, sometimes you are. Fact is that many of these companies have set up in India! Now that's the best!

Try and explain your medical insurance claim problem to someone in New Delhi.

Scary thing is that a manager had to have had something to do with it. You need to wonder who the hell hires the manager. That's the part that frightens me the most. It's that trickle-down effect to obscurity. People that shouldn't have any power being put into a position of power, feeling powerful, and actually having the authority to hire dweebs that have some authority. OUCH! Anyway, this all makes it so much easier for us peddlers.

A year or so ago, I needed to buy a new computer. Now, that's a pretty good-sized investment. I went to three stores, Best Buy, Comp USA, and Circuit City. I must let you know a minor point (being sarcastic here) … it was Christmastime. So, if the sales floors were ever staffed, this was it. Right? Well, they were staffed all right, but getting one of those so-called "salespeople" to wait on me was another story. I spent 30 minutes in the first store, looking at computers, seeing the salespeople hanging around doing nothing, and left without anyone asking if I needed help. The second store was the same deal. This time, the "boys" were playing computer games, which was obviously much more important than me and my requirements. Then I went to Circuit City, and, low and behold, it happened again. As they say, *same deal, another store.* At least that's what I've changed the expression to for now. As I was leaving, convinced I was going to go on-line to order, a manager (?) asked if someone had taken care of me. I could not resist. I unloaded. Basically, I told him that if I had my druthers (that means a choice), I would open a store right next to his and sell computers and electronics. I'd become filthy rich. All I would have to do is greet the customer and try to help. *Now isn't that a unique approach?* I went on to explain how appalling it was, especially to me, that he, as a manager, would stand by and watch the people he hired do absolutely nothing. I was, in fact, a paying customer, in need of a computer. All I wanted was to have someone sell me one. Here's the worst part … After unloading on this guy for ten minutes (and he was the chief in charge), he simply said, "I'm sorry" and he let me leave. He didn't even offer to help me. He didn't even try to save the sale. The idiot (sorry, but what else could I possibly call him?) didn't even understand after all that was said, and again, he was in charge! What a joke. I would have had this guy (that's me) in the checkout line so fast with the biggest, baddest computer anyone ever saw. And to make it even worse, they seem to stay in business. Something is terribly wrong here.

For the purpose of this chapter, let's assume the management is pretty good and they hired capable salespeople. So now, we have these guys and gals who have the talent to sell something. Some have more education than others. Let me put that theory to rest right now. Education is nice to have, but it rarely makes much of a difference on the street where sales are made.

Another steady factor, consistent through my career, is that more education rarely, if ever, means more sales. In fact, sad to say, the highly educated guy or gal with all the degrees usually gets the old butt kicked in a pure sales environment. Anyway, that's getting off the subject. I already told you that I dropped out of school to sell something. I'm definitely not the example you want to show your kids of someone who hit the old books. That is not the role model I want to be.

Getting back to the point, Mr. Gibbs was trying to say that after the talent is taken for granted, it's the smarts that make it all work. In football, it's how the playbook is read and implemented. In sales, it's how the playbook is read and implemented. Different subject matter, different playbooks, but same scenario. Again, the talent is a "given." It's execution, another word for "smarts," that makes the difference.

So many times through the years, I saw raw talent, rough around the edges, kick butt. Guess I was one of them. I could not articulate it like the "big guys," but believe me, I lost very few sales. I guarantee that I never lost a sale to a big vocabulary … NEVER!

I remember a great story that sticks, even after all these years. When I first got into the Rep business, I was living in a four-season climate. As you know, with four seasons comes snow, cold, and the need for heaters. As a new Rep, I was fortunate enough to get this line of portable heaters, and I made a call on a local chain of home centers. This was before the huge influx of the mass merchandisers we see today. Companies like Lowe's, Home Depot, and so forth were not around. Instead, local companies with a few stores were the "big" deals.

Anyway, I made an appointment, loaded up my stuff, and went to see the buyer. While waiting, I sat in the lobby and overheard two other Reps talking (remember how much you can learn in a lobby). Guess what they were talking about? You got it, heaters!

One Rep, his name was John, was Rep Numero Uno in town. Some would tell you that he "owned" the account. (By the way, never ever use that expression. Nobody owns an account. I must admit, at certain points in my career, I came pretty close. But in reality, you are only as good as the last presentation.) So, the buyer was a bit late. "Well-known, power-hitting" John was called in before me. He had this relationship with the buyer, which was apparent when they decided to stop in the lounge for coffee on the way to the office. John was, as I saw it, the articulate, first-round pick. Here I was, the schlep from Chicago with a new line of heaters who just knew he was going to take the business from John. You know why? Because I was smarter than him. First, smart guys don't talk in public places in front of people that they don't know, people that could be the competition. Next, smart guys take nothing for granted, cocky guys do. The smart guy (that was me) pretends that he's not listening by reading a magazine (actually looking at the pictures) while listening intently to every word.

By the time John went in to the buyer's office, I was on the phone to my manager in Wisconsin, giving him the info I had just heard. By the time I was finished, I was able to take John's program apart, piece by piece. I knew exactly what I had to do. I read my playbook and was able to tailor it to the competition. I came in as a salesman, no banter, no bullshit, and no reason to try to be his pal. He already had John. It was my job to make him money. The rest is history.

Later on, I got to know John. We became pretty good friends, although I always felt that he had me in a pretty careful place because he could never figure out, as smart as he thought he was, how I got that heater business away from him. He just couldn't believe it. And, my friends, that was only the beginning. I took all kinds of sales and several lines from John. The buyer, his name was John too, and I had many cups of coffee together after that. In fact, I put the buyer in the Rep business. He wound up working for me. Strange things happen when you're not too smart!

Here's the point: You can have all the talent in the world, but if you do not know how to use it correctly, you will fail. Think for a minute (back to football) of all the Heisman Trophy winners that failed in the NFL. For those who may not know, the Heisman Trophy is awarded annually to the best college football player in the country. It's a very big deal, but most Heisman winners do not achieve pro football stardom. They get the big draft, the big contract, but rarely do they shine. Does that say something about this subject? On the other hand, how many third- or fourth-round picks wind up being superstars? Think of Joe Montana as your first example!

I knew a kid many years ago who was a salesman for the company I worked for. It was my first sales job, and when I joined the company, all I could hear was talk about Tony P (that was his name) and what a great talent he was. He had this degree and that degree and could do this and do that.

Here I was, a raw rookie who, as you already know, had some education but not like this Tony P. I was in awe even before I met him. He was in my region and our paths crossed soon after I joined the company. Good old Tony P, cocky as hell, full of himself in front of the new kid. Little did he know that I was going to kick his ass. Little did he know, but I knew; never had any doubt at all. I knew that in spite of it all, I was much smarter than the "first-round pick" and that one of us was going to get the BIG job down the road.

I knew what I had to do. I had to work smarter, go the extra mile, and get the unexpected done. While he was doing the typical, expected stuff that *he was hired for,* as we all were, old Lee was out doing things that nobody expected to get done. Instead of calling on "typical" accounts, I tried to find other ways of making sales. We were in the label-maker business, so I went to Industrial User and set up labeling and organizational procedures for them. One of these users was Lockheed Aircraft, another was Hughes Aircraft. I need to note that this extra effort ultimately developed into what is now known as OSHA, a government agency that, among other things, still uses my labeling program as a mandatory procedure for every factory.

I knew, early on, that I would not be successful with traditional accounts and traditional expectations. I had to use my brain and develop business. I also made an extra effort on reports. Mine were always typed (not the norm in those days; no word processors) and consisted of clear answers, as well as lots of extra stuff. Suddenly, the tables were turned. I was head of the sales heap, and everyone in management was talking about me, not Tony P. I didn't think about what was expected, focusing only on the unexpected. I did whatever I could to get the job done, expected or not. You know, Tony could not figure it out. Through the years, I met dozens of Tony Ps, and in every case, the outcome was the same. NO CONTEST!

Well, no reason to end it here. My first sales job was in the office products industry. I began as a salesman and became the National Sales Manager in a few short years. It didn't happen because of anything other than my ability to hit the streets, use my senses, and get the business, which, as you will soon learn in sales, any sales, is all that matters. When all the facts are gathered and all the dice are thrown, it's the guy or gal who *writes the most business that makes the most money and ultimately gets the most respect.*

As for Tony P, he just could not bring himself to work for me. He just couldn't see it. So Tony P was fired by guess who. I replaced him, though, quite readily and easily, I might add. As for Joe Gibbs, he doesn't have too many Tony P's on his field. He trades them for guys that go the extra mile and think about what they need to do to get the job done … get the ball into the end zone. The good old end zone, which is no different than the good old purchase order.

Good luck, Joe. See you at the Super Bowl.

MLM

It sounds like a disease or long-term illness. Maybe it is in some ways. MLM is Multi-Level Marketing. I would be terribly remiss if I did not devote some time (small amount preferably) to this subject. After all, as ludicrous as this seems to me, some of you might actually be thinking that this is a form of sales and it is legit.

At some point, you will get a call from a friend you know very well or someone you hardly know who was recommended by someone you know very well. He or she will have "*the opportunity of a lifetime for you*" and will ask for only a few minutes of your time. They may add that "*this few minutes may change your whole life.*" Welcome to the world of MLM. Those of us who are smart will ask the caller right away if this *few minutes* deals with an MLM. If they say yes or if they give you the old hem and haw (that means yes without admitting it), make every excuse in the world to avoid a meeting. You do not want to do this.

Multi-level marketing is not a new concept. In fact, it's been around a very long time and has had a few other names, names that have changed to protect the concept from bordering on the illegal. Anyway, today it's MLM, and I suppose it's been changed enough to be a safe, legal concept. To me, it's a great big scam and as much of an insult as calling the sale of a creme-filled donut "sales". And you know how I feel about that.

One of my close relatives came to me one day after having been at a meeting (there will always be meetings for MLMs) and having been duly impressed. It was sad because he was so excited after hearing the presentation the night before from the slick, well-dressed (Armani only) representative who actually showed checks depicting how little he made two years ago versus the enormous amount of money he was making now. It was kind of like the diet ads showing this obese person and the same poor soul a few months later, all svelte and beautiful. How amazing. Everyone needs to try these diet pills or whatever the hell it is they are selling by showing this comparison. It was the same for my poor relative. *"Hey, I actually met this guy that was broke two years ago. He showed us his check on an overhead projector. Then, after two years, you should see how much he is making. This fella is taking home $50,000 or $60,000 a month. Lee, I saw the friggin checks."*

How was I going to break the news to my overwhelmed family member? How could I convince him that it was a setup? I was afraid to burst his balloon. Should I do it or not? Well, he asked my advice and I feared he was probably about to ask me for a loan. I was compelled to go for it.

I started by asking simple questions, *"Would you ever go to work for a company that did not have an interview process? A company that did not have a selection procedure? Doesn't every company have some hiring standards?"* The answer to all of these was obvious. If you join a company, you do so after you decide you want them and they decide they want you. It's a selection process. Every company has one, whether it's a line cook position at Denny's, a newspaper route, or a pharmaceutical sales job. All companies have a selection process. That's what resumes are for, right? Wrong! How was I supposed to tell old innocence here that the presentation he saw was one that went on every week (sometimes two or three times a week) in every imaginable city and that anyone, absolutely anyone, who wanted to join the company could. In other words, if you could breathe and stand upright, you were in. Well, maybe having to stand upright is going too far. They would probably hire bedridden people. The breathing part was, in reality, all that was necessary. What does that tell you? The guy you saw with all the money? He was a setup. Literally one in a million. He was there at the very beginning. I even told him the questions that were asked:

> *Where do you see yourself two years from now?*
> *What do you want for your family?*
> *Are you tired of making everyone else money?*
> *Are there people you know who would like to become rich?*
> *What if I could change all of that?*

My relative asked, "Hey, Lee, how did you know all those questions?"

Because they are the same ones used at every MLM meeting, of which there are literally thousands every week of the year. Ask someone if they want to get rich. What are they going to say? Try it on some poor schlep who is making minimum wage. Even he can get in on the deal for the same price as you. Anyone can join and start "selling" (ouch) immediately. All you have to do is buy the starter pack and start bringing folks to meetings.

When it first began, it was called "Pyramid Marketing," but that soon became an obvious scheme and the government stopped it. But it's still the same. Different day, but same scheme. It's basically a pyramid. Things build on top of things. And when it's presented properly, it's so impressive, and, boy oh boy, is it ever tempting. They talk about building an organization (and who doesn't want to build their own organization?) They call it a "line." The line grows and so do you. Here's the concept…

> You buy the deal, then you sell it to someone else (give them the opportunity). You now make money on your sales and the new guy's as well. Sounds great, huh? But that's just the beginning. Now, the new guy sells it to another person, maybe ten people, who sell it to ten more people, who sell it to ten more people. Pretty soon, you have thousands of people working for you and all you have to do is sit on your ass and collect the checks because you get a piece of everyone's sales. Why? Because you started the whole thing by giving the first guy, who gave the next guy (etc., etc.), the chance to get rich. They are all getting rich. You are a regular philanthropist. Keep it up. The MLM Humanitarian Award awaits you!

If the "line" keeps going for a few years, you are done!

There is only one problem with this. It doesn't work! Other than that, it's terrific.

The one thing that is consistent about every one of these things is the cases of samples you paid for that are in your garage. It's called a *Starter Kit,* but in reality, it's a bunch of junk. But they got you to pay money for it. Try to return it. No way!

And because of all your enthusiasm, you've probably lost all of your friends. In order to even have the slightest chance of success, you must present this "opportunity of a lifetime" to every breathing person you have ever known. The idea is to get them to the meetings so that they can see Slick in his Armani suit firsthand. They will also buy and be an integral part of your "line" and have samples of their own in their garage. Your job is to make an appointment with every single person you know, successful or not, and make a pitch. *"Where do you see yourself five years from now?"* will be your most-used sentence. You will alienate everyone you know, piss people off, and find that most people begin to avoid you like the plague. They have heard the spiel 300 times before and have been given the opportunity. You become a boring sales guy that everyone wants to avoid and turn off. If you happen to find a poor soul or two that signs up, they will wind up hating you for life because they will fail and it's your damn fault. Wonder why us peddlers get a bad name?

Don't get me wrong, there are some success stories, but they are few and far between. The money has been made by the folks at the top. The enthusiastic so-called friend, looking out for your future with this unbelievable opportunity, will fail. The next time you see him or her, he or she will be talking about something else and will have some illogical excuse for the failure just endured. My conclusion: You'd be far better off saving your money and buying a donut shop.

SO ... WHAT DO I NEED TO DO TO MAKE YOU HAPPY?

"Don't weigh the yogurt"

Here I am, wrapping this thing up and putting the final touches on this ten-year project, when something happens that compels me to write one more chapter. I know you've heard that before, but at some point (soon, I hope), I will be through and the publisher can deal with my disgruntled fans.

In the meantime, I would be remiss if I did not include my most recent experience in this writing. It involves the automobile industry, and I will admit, I have been less than complimentary about that industry. After all, in far too many cases, rookies are hired with little or no experience and put out to "sell" us the second-most-expensive purchase most of us will ever make. It's one of the reasons I refer to selling donuts as a title to this book. In all fairness, I have met a few great car salesmen in my life, one being one of my favorite peddlers (remember, that's what I am), Lee Iacocca.

I have purchased, leased, or been involved in the purchase of at least 100 cars through the years. When I look for a car today, I usually skip the bullshit and go directly to the sales manager, or, if possible, his boss. It seems to fit me better and keeps the poor sales guy from putting up with me. I'm pretty tough, I admit. I have probably driven at least three or four "pretenders" into another industry. Probably telephone solicitation or multi-level marketing of some sort.

I have spent the last few days delighted at watching someone in the car industry work. Someone who made me feel that dollars and profit were not his motivation, but instead and far more importantly, my happiness was the only thing that mattered. This is rare in any business, but when we're talking about $80,000 or so, it's probably non-existent. Basically, here's what happened. My wife leased a car 1,500 miles ago. This week it stopped running and had to be towed. That happens, I guess, but it only added to the real point that she really was not happy with the car from day one. Sure, it had a slight mechanical problem that could probably be worked out, but the car, which is a very expensive convertible, had no "magic" in my wife's eyes. In other words, we needed to get out of it, plain and simple! It just wasn't right. So, adding the fact that it had to be towed and the other fact that the parts were not readily available to make it drivable, I found it to be an opportunity to vent and I called the top guy, the manager at the dealership.

I explained the frustrations we were having and my wife's unhappiness with the car overall. This vehicle was only a few months old and only had 1,500 miles on it. At the same time, I know the business well enough to realize that this car is a used car now.

The manager, Bob (that's as far as I will go), listened to my presentation of my spouse's unhappiness and said, *"WHAT DO I NEED TO DO TO MAKE YOU HAPPY?"* Imagine that for a unique approach to solving problems! I told him that ideally, another car in the right color would be the ultimate objective. He said, *"IF THAT'S WHAT IT WILL TAKE TO KEEP YOU AS A HAPPY CUSTOMER, THEN LET ME SEE WHAT I CAN DO."*

The rest of the story is not all that important. The fact is that Bob made it happen. Stacy is getting a brand new car, in the color she wants, with more equipment on it than she had before, with absolutely no increase in price or penalty to us. He even paid the freight because he had to find the car in another state and had to ship it in. I should add that when we agreed to the original car, we were told that transport was not an option because it "was too expensive and that the only car available on the lot was the one we got. Guess I should have confirmed that with Bob.

I've been around long enough and my credentials will safely allow me to consider myself a sales professional. I've been very successful, and one of the reasons I have always succeeded (and always will) is the fact that the word "NO" is not and never has been a part of my vocabulary. It just doesn't exist.

Years ago, I became quite appalled when watching the owner of a yogurt store weigh my yogurt on a scale. I told my wife that if we ever happened to own a place where weight mattered, we would never, never weigh anything. As you know, I own a restaurant and there never will be a scale anywhere within eyesight of any customer. I consider it a cheap insult. So, every employee that is ever hired hears the story about the yogurt years ago and learns what *"don't weigh the yogurt"* means.

It really goes further than that. The real bottom line is to never let the customer feel like you care about the money. Never talk about profit, margins, portions, etc. In my restaurant, the word "no" is never used. The customer gets whatever he or she wants and the portion size means nothing. When they leave my place, the last thing they think I thought about was money. And that is exactly what Bob did at Jaguar. I have no idea what corporate Jaguar did, if anything. I have no idea what Bob really had to do. All I know is that he did whatever it took to make us happy. He never "weighed the yogurt," at least not in front of me. He certainly could have, like most would have, explained the "profit thing" to me and how hard it would be to take a sold car back with no penalty. He could have hemmed, hawed, and whined. He could have turned his back. I don't really know the whole deal, but what I do know is that I met a true professional who has my business and will have it for a long time, as well as my recommendation to anyone I can give it to.

Business is pretty simple. We screw it up by making it difficult. The money will take care of itself if we take care of the customer. So many owners and salespeople just can't seem to figure that out. That's why it's so easy for some of us to kick the proverbial butts of our competitors. I am citing this example because it means something. It teaches us something about operating in the sales jungle. "What do I have to do to make you happy?"

IT JUST DOESN'T GET SIMPLER THAN THAT!

Thanks, Bob.

THE GUY WITH THE GREEN HAIR

Don't go out and dye your hair before I tell you what I really mean here. There will be times that you will not be able to get the business (as we say), no matter what you do or how hard you try. It won't matter … pricing, programs, superior goods. You ain't gonna get it. Yes, it happened to me. Not often, but it did happen. Nothing is more frustrating to a peddler.

Here's a great example, one that I will never forget. I was selling plush (stuffed animals) to a very big retailer. It was a warehouse club account. The volume was huge. A company that I represented in China would "knock goods off." That meant that they would take merchandise manufactured by a well-known, major manufacturer and copy it exactly for a fraction of the cost, making it a great bargain. Don't be shocked. Things are knocked off all the time. Where do you think all these bargains come from? This worked great for warehouse clubs because the entire concept is based on value. For example, a teddy bear manufactured by a big, well-known manufacturer was sold to major retailers for $49.95. We could take the exact bear and make it available at this warehouse club (exact one) for $14.95. We sold tens of thousands of them. At one point, we sold so many of a big gorilla that I thought we had sold one to every customer in America. I used to see these guys in back windows of cars, on the back of Harleys, everywhere. Great value, great price, and very big money for me.

Suddenly, the account changes buyers and *she* decides that this multi-million dollar, no-brainer, nothing-but-profit program isn't working. I am basically on a "carte blanche" deal with these guys. The more goods I could get, the more I could deliver.

Not only am I making a fortune, but so are they. This was in "Rep's heaven" and along comes Mary with a better idea. She begins looking for a better value. <u>Trust me, there is no better value</u>. There cannot be a better value. We are giving the stuff away and the quality is unbelievable. Everyone in the industry is trying to figure it out. They are calling me every day to get goods, but I simply cannot get any more made. We are selling that many. I had to turn down business for heaven's sake! But she thinks she can do better. I am told that she has no experience in the area. In fact, she was a buyer for disposables (paper plates) previously. Doesn't that make perfect sense? What a brilliant decision. She is negative from the very start. This is almost where you get to know what the green hair means. So, I decide to take her head-on. I get an idea. It has to work. I take her and her boss, the Merchandise Manager, a good friend of mine named Scott, to lunch at a local shopping center. One of the stores at the center is FAO Schwartz, which is the world's most renowned and most respected toy store. It sets the trends, gets the hottest goods, and leads the industry. We all agree on the way over there that if FAO has it and says that it's "hot," then it must be. I give the buyer my credit card, telling her to buy whatever she wanted with it so we could have a sample. I go with Scott to shop around for a while, leaving her alone. No budget is set. She can spend what she wants. Then, she is to give me the items and I would send those very items to China for duplication, exactly as they were, only at a fraction of the cost. We are so excited at the possibility of what we can produce here. Scott and I are drooling with anticipation. I say, "Hey, Scott, *this is almost illegal.*"

Guess what? She could not find anything that she felt would be suitable. What? At FAO Schwartz? Please, this must be a joke. Even her boss was dumbfounded. I couldn't believe it. I said to myself, "Are you kidding me? You couldn't find one single item at FAO Schwartz?" As you can imagine, that was the end of the program, at least as far as I was concerned. Trying to better herself with so-called "reps" that she said she knew quite well, the buyer failed miserably. By the time Scott and the boys came back to me to get it back on track, it was too late. There was only so much plush that I could get. By the time the customer realized that they had a goof on their hands, the goods were sold elsewhere. The program was gone and so was a quarter of a million dollars in commission.

At one point during all this, I had a discussion with the president of a major company that I was representing. This guy was a legend and knew the industry better than anyone I ever knew. I really respected him, and to this very day, I consider him one of the very best. He laughed when I told him about the FAO Schwartz fiasco and he said, "It's the green hair thing." Puzzled, I asked him to explain. He told me that the buyer was rarely, if ever, totally objective (boy, if that's not an understatement). If he/she did not like you for any reason, there would be very little chance of getting the business. In other words, as he put it, "If the buyer likes the guy with the green hair, the guy with the green hair will prevail." It was his GREEN HAIR theory. He even admitted that he hired Reps based on relationships most of the time. He was always looking for the guy with the green hair to represent him. I found this to be quite true, quite often. In fact, thankfully, I was the guy with the green hair most of the time. But when I wasn't, too bad!

One time, I went full circle with a buyer named Charlene Roberts. I mention her name because I hope that someday she reads this. That's if some salesman hasn't erupted during one of her appointments and dumped her in the lake somewhere. She arrived at this particular account with a terrible reputation of being very tough to deal with. Well, she thought I was the guy with the green hair. We became fast friends and, oh boy, did she lay the purchase orders on me. If I presented it, she bought it. It went on like that for a while (not long enough). That is, until I did something to piss her off. It was over nothing ... the fact that I had to say no about a personal favor. She turned 180 degrees. In a matter of about 24 hours, I was done. I couldn't even get appointments. She turned on me like a bad meal. It got so bad that it began costing the account lots of dough. So, at a very appropriate time (at a ball game with the VP of marketing for the company), I took the opportunity to vent. He brought it up, asking how I was doing with Charlene. This guy and I were friends, and so, when I told him that I was turned off like a faucet, he couldn't believe it. He told me that he asked her if she was buying goods from Lee and she said that she was. What a laugh. In fact, I broke up. So, I made him a deal. I told him about the green hair theory. By this time, we were done with the game. We were in dessert mode, which was usually Cognac with this fella.

I told him that I'd bet that I could bring Charlene an undeliverable deal. A price that was below cost and one that even I could never get through the factory. It would be so low that she would have to take it, only SHE WOULDN'T.

The erroneous deal, which I let my VP friend help me put together, was the lowest price ever offered in that category, which was, I must add, a huge category (TRASH BAGS). He went along with it, checking with me every day or so to see if I made the presentation. Hell, I couldn't even get the appointment. I finally did. Guess what? She didn't even want to see the price. She turned it down flat. I told her that it was the strongest deal ever offered and she said, "We'll have to live without it," and promptly walked out of the room. Boy, did she hate my brown hair! And just because I said no! I won my bet and couldn't wait to tell Mr. VP. The green hair theory prevailed again. I didn't have it so I didn't get it. Simple as that. In case you're interested, good old Charlene had to find new employment a few short days later. And guess what? I didn't even have to dye my hair.

BORN WITH THE SILVER SPOON

This may be a hell of a good time to slow this down a bit and take you all back in time because, before you get carried away with all this unbelievable success I have enjoyed (remember, I am a dropout), you ought to know that it wasn't always like this.

First of all, forget the silver spoon. There wasn't any. I grew up in a great home, but there sure wasn't any wealth. Dad worked hard, but never forgot the depression and all that went with it. When I was very young, we lived on the west side of Chicago in an apartment building that had three floors occupied by us, my grandparents, and my aunt and uncle. It was one hell of a rough neighborhood. Being the only Jewish family in it, we got used to getting the shit beat out of us regularly. No other way to say it. Boy, could I tell you some stories, but I won't. I guess, however, that the abuse did help me to work a little harder and appreciate things a bit more. When I was in kindergarten, we moved to a better area, taking our bruises (some still hanging around) with us.

I remember how much we appreciated our own rooms, a porch to sit on at night (mosquitoes and all), and a lawn to mow. We even had a one-car garage. It was the big-time to us. I walked to school with other kids, some even Jewish. I had a home. Still, we had to work for what we had. I get such a kick out of my kids today who are so picky about what they wear and where they shop. When I was a young boy, my dad went to visit my uncle who had a shoe store about 60 miles out of Chicago. He'd go there about three times a year and he would bring me back shoes. I had no choice but to wear them in spite of the fact that they were damn ugly. Somehow, he had a way of picking the most awful shoes. I couldn't throw them out because Dad paid for them. So, I went to school in these ugly Oxfords. That's the way it was. I must have been pretty embarrassed since I still remember it 50 years later. But at least I had some new shoes, as ugly as they were. He thought they looked pretty good though. He'd tell me over and again what great shoes they were, what a great deal Uncle Max gave him, and how great they looked on my feet. Most important was the fact that these beauties would last forever. Oh, good! The amazing part of the whole thing was that he was totally convinced that I would have picked the same shoes had I gone with him. You bet, Dad! Clothes were not much different although, thank the Lord, I didn't have a relative in the clothing business. There was more than one occasion that an old shirt or pair of pants was taken from the trash and fixed as "good as new."

For lack of a better term, let's call this the "Silver Spoon Syndrome." I have been fortunate enough to enjoy great success, and I guess the idea of having shoes bought for me was an inspiration for the future.

That's why my expectations for the Rep business were not all that high. The Rep is the independent contractor that we talked about, representing various manufacturers, selling to the trade on a straight-commission basis. Sure, I knew that I was going to do well and make a lot of money. I also knew that I had to eat from the beginning and so my expectations could not be too high, at least to start.

Factoring in the fact that I became one of the industry's most successful Reps, representing some of the biggest, best-known names in the world, it would be awfully hard to believe what I started out with. The big lines (Canon, Fuji, Mobil, AT&T) came later, after a great deal of work and the development of a track record. To start, I had to sell something that would generate cash flow. I had a family and I needed the money. So, I found two items. The first, believe it or not, was this thing called the "Laffin Head." Told you you'd have a hard time believing it. Let me describe this to you. Picture an ugly, very ugly, old man's face, all wrinkled and shriveled up. It's probably the ugliest face you have ever seen. This face has a scarf around his neck and a hat. It hangs on the wall with a bow tie hanging that says, *"Pull Me."* When you do, <u>it spits at you</u> (usually right in the face) and starts laughing like crazy. It actually belly laughs. That's the item and that's how I started in the Rep business. Not with AT&T, but with the Laffun Head. I went to small stores of various types and sold this ridiculous-looking thing. Guess what?! I made a lot of money. I sold the crap out of it. It made me a living.

That led to the second biggie. I got a line of key chains that looked like cowboy boots. They came on a rack and I sold them to every conceivable type of retailer. I made a lot more money. Between the two items, I did pretty damn well. But, a silver spoon? It was more like a shovel full of dog crap! And to think, all this led to my big-time in the business.

I remember after I had experienced and built a successful business (Rep) and I had a warehouse and everything, my sweet wife walked through it one day and said that she had one hell of a hard time trying to find anything that she would want to take home with her. I understood. I told her that if I could keep selling this garbage, she could shop anywhere she wanted to.

I guess the moral of the story has something to do with the fact that a peddler can sell anything as long as there is someone to sell it to. It doesn't matter what it is. It just depends on whose sample case the stuff is in. And I know a lot of guys who actually did start with the old "Silver Spoon." They had great, well-known lines in their bag right from the start, not earned, but given or inherited. Usually they fell on their proverbial asses. SOMETIMES, SILVER HAS TO BE EARNED.

THE END

It's taken me ten years, off and on (mostly off), to get this done or at least to a point that I feel I should end it. Frankly, it's getting too serious. As you may have guessed, my entire career has been built on a rather light sense of humor.

I have tried to have fun all along the way, and, thank the good Lord, I have. Now I have completed this little book. I have no idea what it will become, if anything. My hope is that it may find its way into the hands of a few and serve as a guide, of sorts, to helping those who understand me, to understand the zany world of selling. It's a proud profession and one that I am proud to have been a part of.

As for you, it's hard to describe, but I can (in a way) see your faces. Writing this has given me the chance to know some of you in a strange sort of way. We all want, or wanted, the very same things and we have so much in common. I wish you luck and, above all else, happiness.

ABOUT THE AUTHOR

Lee Klein has been in the field of Sales and Marketing for over thirty-five years. His experience includes positions on a national sales and management level, sales training and consultation, marketing consultation/management, product development and as an advisor for major corporations as well as owning and operating his own companies, sales agencies and businesses. He has been affiliated with such worldwide companies as AT&T, Canon, Mobil Oil, Panasonic, Newell Corporation, Fuji, Samsung and their various divisions.

He has received many professional and highly coveted awards designated for excellence and outstanding service in several industries. He has been instrumental in market development of several, internationally known, successful products and companies and has, throughout his career, sat on The Governing Boards of companies and has served on The Advisory Council of several major corporations.

Lee currently resides in Scottsdale, Arizona and is still active in the daily operation of his businesses. He recently completed his book, Serving Donuts is not Sales, that focuses on his experiences and very strong beliefs as they relate to Sales, specifically the perception, the responsibility and role of the salesman, as a professional in the Business World.

www.ingramcontent.com/pod-product-compliance
Lightning Source LLC
Chambersburg PA
CBHW030008190526
45157CB00014B/1206